# THE
# ENGLISH
## AT
# TABLE

THE

# ENGLISH

AT

# TABLE

## DIGBY ANDERSON

With foreword by
CHARLES MOORE

and illustrations by
MICHAEL HEATH

THE
SOCIAL
AFFAIRS
UNIT

Printed and bound in the United Kingdom

ISBN 1-904863-18-3

Social Affairs Unit
314-322 Regent Street
London W1B 5SA
www.socialaffairsunit.org.uk

# CONTENTS

# ACKNOWLEDGEMENTS

My wife, Judith Anderson, is responsible for much
that is best and most virulent in these pages.

# THE AUTHOR

Social critic Dr Digby Anderson has been a regular columnist for *The Times*, *Sunday Times* and the *Sunday Telegraph*. He was for fifteen years food columnist at the *Spectator* and, in the USA, at *National Review*. His books include *The Spectator Book of Imperative Cooking*, a study of friendship entitled *Losing Friends* and *All Oiks Now: The Unnoticed Surrender of Middle England*. He lives, shops, cooks and eats with his wife in the Buckinghamshire countryside and the Kent seaside, and wherever in Latin countries he can find markets and a kitchen and dining room to rent.

# FOREWORD

Editors always feel very proud when they help launch a new talent on the world, and I can claim to have done this with Digby Anderson. To be sure, Digby was already well known as a social scientist, but it was I who persuaded him, more than 20 years ago, to write about food in the pages of the *Spectator*, where he began a column called 'Imperative Cooking'.

In Digby's case, however, my pride is tinged with some guilt. There is no doubt about the brilliance of what he writes, nor about his knowledge of the subject; but did I let loose upon the world a force so powerful and so frightening that the British cook, on reading him, will suffer a nervous breakdown in the face of his onslaught?

The answer is, unequivocally, yes.

The author shows no mercy towards the short cuts, over-elaboration, laziness, squeamishness, incompetence, cowardice, ingratitude and numerous other vices which, he believes, the British exhibit when we cook, or pretend to cook. If we are what we eat, then we British are very bad indeed.

Digby notices our strange love of pumping everything full of water, our erroneous belief that a picnic may only be eaten out of doors, and our readiness to exchange the old-fashioned bad cooking of the 1950s for an even worse (because more pretentious) modern sort of cuisine (e.g. replacing the honestly dreary marrow with the dishonestly disgusting courgette). He details how we have destroyed breakfast, the one meal in which we once led the world. He exposes what he says is the lie that vegetarian food can be as interesting as meat and fish. In short, he carves up the English cook as expertly as he carves every last piece of flesh off a bird.

And the terrible thing about all this is that Digby Anderson is right. Cooking does depend first and foremost on ingredients. It does require the skills of the quartermaster.

It does need very frequent shopping, and requires pleasure to be taken in that frequency. It does require the possession of stocks, and the getting to grips with carcasses, though what Digby calls 'the deep pleasure at that moment when your hand has felt its way up a fat duck's bottom' is probably not, even in his view, compulsory.

Digby Anderson brings to the subject two things that give him authority. The first is his superb personal knowledge of everything to do with food, his unquestioning devotion to the facts of the matter. The second is his understanding that what he is talking about is something big which goes beyond the ingredients. It has to do with tradition, morality, family, religion and national culture. If all these are scorned, though our stomachs may well be full, our deep hunger is unappeased.

This book is also very funny. Like all books that make you laugh a lot, it is also extremely serious.

*Charles Moore*

*[I]n the latter times some shall depart from the faith giving heed to seducing spirits and doctrines of devils. Speaking lies in hypocrisy…commanding to abstain from meats, which God has created to be received with thanksgiving. For every creature is good and nothing is to be refused.*
First Epistle of Paul the Apostle to Timothy (Ch 4 verses 1–3)

*In the world to come a man will have to face judgement for every legitimate pleasure which he denied himself.*
Jerusalem Talmud, Kiddushin 4:12

*A lot of people in France do not realise that British food is excellent.*
Lady Penelope Holmes, wife of the British Ambassador to France, quoted in *The Times*, 13 March 2006

*The Office for National Statistics changes its 650-strong basket of goods and services [most widely bought] once a year to include more up-to-date items…[In 2006] the 'out' list includes the dining room table – because families no longer eat meals together.*
*Daily Telegraph*, 21 March 2006

# CHAPTER I

# A REVOLUTION IN ENGLISH FOOD?

## SOAKED IN MARGATE

There is no land between Margate and the Arctic. When the
north-east wind blows, Northdown Road, which used to be
the main shopping area running from Margate to Cliftonville,
can be very cold indeed. It's worse when it's raining as well. It
was blowing, raining and bitterly cold when I was there late
one morning in 1963. I was looking for a black olive or two.
I knew there weren't any in my own nearby home town of
Broadstairs. In those days most high streets would have been
unable to produce a black olive. You might have been lucky
and found a green one in a tiny jar. It would have been kept
just in case someone wanted to make a cocktail. Since cock-
tails had largely disappeared by the 1960s, any green olive you
did find would have been distinctly squashy and tasteless. If it
had originally been stuffed with a speck of red pepper, this
would have slipped out, to be found – with a cloudy deposit of
disintegrated olives – at the bottom of the jar. Anyhow, I did
not want a green olive; I wanted a black one. Since I wanted
black olives for a dish with only three ingredients, leaving out
the olives was likely to have had far-reaching consequences.

Several of the cafés on the seafront at Margate were
owned by Greek Cypriot families. There were enough Greek
Cypriots in Margate to justify a Greek Orthodox church. The
Cypriots did not serve olives in their cafés. They served fish
and chips, and steaks and roast chicken. But I thought they
might eat the odd black olive themselves and imagined that

there might, somewhere in Margate, be a Greek shop selling vine leaves, aubergines, Greek coffee, olive oil and olives. If there was such a shop, I couldn't find it. After two hours of tramping about in the wind, rain and cold, the best I could find was a Jewish delicatessen. I was very grateful to it. Although it sold nothing else I wanted, it did have black olives – expensive, aged, soft, rather tasteless, but still clearly black olives.

### INGREDIENTS YOU COULDN'T FIND IN THE SIXTIES

That's what it was like in the early sixties – and not just for olives. If you wanted any of the basics of 'Latin' cooking, you had to do a lot of hunting, tramping and getting cold and wet. Except in London, where Brewer Street and Old Compton Street were goldmines, most large towns might have a shop somewhere with these ingredients, but it was often only known to the cognoscenti. Some ingredients could be bought in high-street stores, but only in quantities and at prices that were silly. Olive oil was sold in tiny bottles, probably because, if it was used at all, it was as a medicine. It was priced accordingly.

You could, if desperate enough, go abroad in search of your olive. In those days it took about 14 hours by rail and sea to get to Provence from England. Coming back, I used to take a night train, changing at Lyon (to a train that often had no seat spare), then a bus across Paris, then another train to Calais, then the trudge and queue to the boat, the same at Dover, and so on. I won't pretend I went only for olives, but so scarce were such ingredients in England that any sensible person going to the *Midi* on holiday or for work stocked up on bottles of olive oil, jars of olives, tresses of garlic, *saucisson* and all the other things you couldn't find in England. There were not many people who did this – nor, for that matter, many who trudged, freezing cold, round provincial English towns looking for ingredients. The few who did were regarded as barmy – if they were ever rash enough to relate their forays.

The olives were for a particular dish, versions of which were widely cooked in the South of France. If it has a name I don't know it. There are dishes like it in Elizabeth David's books, but they are a little more complicated. It is marvellous. You take a couple of pounds of stewing beef – use mixed shin and neck – and marinade it in at least a full bottle of wine: in those days one used Algerian red. The beef is then stewed in the wine for two or three hours. It is then removed from the wine and the wine is reduced to two or three tablespoons of concentrated heaven. The meat is thrown back in for a reheat, along with half a pound of olives. No herbs, no garlic, no carrot, no *lardons*, no trotter, no *beurre manié*, no pepper, no salt. No frying of the beef first. It is served with another of the simplest things imaginable – bread fried in lashings of olive oil: 'you mean you've been traipsing around in the freezing Margate rain to make this? You must be mad!'

They did not think me quite so mad when they tasted it. But I cannot recall any of the many people who enjoyed it serving it to me when I ate with them. What they served – this is still the sixties, remember – was a creamy sort of Beef Stroganoff with three vegetables: the more cream one added to a dish the more 'continental' it was supposed to be, and thus the more travelled and sophisticated one was. Only one thing was worse than the cream confections: a fondue evening. No, that's not true: I'd forgotten the cotton-wool taste of rainbow trout with stale almonds.

## NO AUBERGINES, CHILLIES OR GARLIC

In the early sixties you could have spent hours fruitlessly scouring the greengrocers of Margate (or almost anywhere else) for courgettes, okra (except soggy stuff in a tin), aubergines, *petits pois*, Chinese cabbage or fresh beansprouts, Indian tinda and karela, peppers and chillies, mangoes, lychees – or even fresh garlic (the plastic garlic-shaped 'puff' garlic powder dispenser being a recent and popular invention).

The fishmonger of the era would not have had tuna, swordfish, sardines, red mullet, squid (except for use as bait), clams or large prawns. Today, you can buy these and much more in any supermarket – should you be the sort of person who goes to a supermarket. The same contrast also seems to apply to eating out. In the early sixties, Chinese restaurants were few and far between, and Indian even thinner on the ground. Both had enormous but extremely limited menus. Mixed grills, chicken soup and fruit salad still dominated English and what were then mysteriously called 'continental' restaurants. Most pubs sold no food apart from pickled eggs, which were, in any case, more of a decoration; I never saw anyone actually eat one (anyone sober, that is). Unless it was to take tea with scones, cakes etc., the English rarely went out to eat and many meals out were not in restaurants but in hotels.

## THE THREE REVOLUTIONS: IN HOME COOKING, SHOPS AND RESTAURANTS

So, apparently there has been a revolution in English food; a huge upheaval in shops, restaurants and pubs and what we cook in our kitchens and serve on our dinner tables. The commonly accepted view today is that England used to be a culinary desert, whereas now it is diverse and wonderful. Words such as 'variety' and 'colourful' are heavily used by advocates of this view. And 'revolution' is an inadequate word to describe what has taken place. This great change allegedly occurred thanks to three 'revolutions'. The first was a revolution in home cooking, plotted and led by the culinary equivalent of Lenin, Elizabeth David in the early sixties. The author of *French Provincial Cooking*, *A Book of Mediterranean Food* and *Italian Food* introduced English people to the *knowledge* of courgettes, olives, tuna and the rest, and explained what to do with them.

The second was a revolution in the ingredients available in

shops. This came about through increasing affluence and greater opportunities for more people to travel abroad and *experience* the new foods; to see for themselves and taste for themselves what courgettes, olives and tuna were like. There was also immigration, especially from the Indian subcontinent, which produced an 'ethnic' demand in England. The demand was not exactly for a Latin diet, but many of the raw ingredients overlapped – garlic, oil, lemons, peppers, aubergines, rice, etc. The 'Asian' shopkeepers were also entrepreneurs who were quite happy to sell the ingredients of other cuisines, such as that of the West Indians. They rapidly took over from the Jewish delicatessens as the source of anything exotic. Once they had done the pioneering work and demand was established, the supermarkets joined in.

The third revolution was in the restaurant and the pub, and it occurred somewhat later, in the eighties and nineties. Pubs started serving food, and then specializing in various types of food. The humblest pub now offered courgettes, possibly under a cheddar coat, and served up (thanks to the recent revolutionary progress in comprehensive education) with an apostrophe: *gratin de courgette's*. Restaurants moved into the various ethnic cuisines, adapted and fused them, possibly creating the odd dish of their own – or even, it was claimed, a new cuisine, British cooking. And there was not a roast chicken in sight. This was all to meet the tastes of the newly affluent, food-wise middle classes – as were the new celebrity chefs. The revolutions reached their pinnacle when they became a central part of television output.

## REVOLUTIONS PERHAPS, BUT NOT NECESSARILY FOR THE BETTER

The conventional view is that the revolutions have led to a massive change for the better in what the English cook and eat. *It is not true.* The changes have indeed been far-reaching, but the self-congratulatory judgement that this change is one very much for the better is nonsense. Food was far from totally awful before the sixties and it is definitely not wonderful now. If there ever *was* a good time, at least for shopping and home cooking, it was probably during the late sixties, when the best of the old era co-existed with the best of the new, and when the new had not been dumbed down to cater to those who eat for fashion's sake.

The facts about the change in the number and type of vegetables and fish in the shops are correct. Who could deny that olives are everywhere today, or that fashions such as those for the *mange tout* or kiwi fruit have, in their heyday, been not just ubiquitous but more or less compulsory? However, some ingredients have also disappeared. In 1963, I had no difficulty finding the beef for my beef in wine. I could go to any one of several local butchers, all of whom either slaughtered their own beasts or knew where the bought-in meat had come from. The butcher would cut me the exact types of meat I wanted: some neck and some shin. But he was replaced by a butcher who didn't know his neck from his shin, and who knew nothing about hanging meat. He was then replaced by another who served pre-cut meat and wore a funny hat. The last local butcher's shop is now shut, and I have to drive eight miles to get good meat and a knowledgeable butcher – precisely twice as far as I had to drive to find a black olive in Margate.

I recently went to Guildford to visit the grave of an old friend. It was raining, as it always is in cemeteries. Guildford is now a substantial and rich city with many inhabitants of taste and wealth. Walking along the main street I saw lots of shops: three bookshops, clothes shops with high-class brands such as 'Jaeger', expensive shoe shops and restaurants. I stopped by a man selling flowers from a stall. Knowing I would be late back home, I thought I would do some shopping in the town. I asked the flower seller for the best, old-fashioned butcher in Guildford: 'There is no butcher in Guildford.' There was no butcher of any kind, good or bad, except a stall on the market on Fridays or Saturdays: 'People go to the supermarket. There's no fishmonger either.'

That is the sort of food revolution England has achieved. I have never seen a full inventory of the good things we have lost in the great British food revolution, but I do remember that whenever I went to Margate my father would remind me to bring home some 'flead cakes' – a pastry made with pork fat. The flead cakes and the shop that sold them are long gone. When I went a couple of miles to Ramsgate I had always to bring back some saveloys. The original saveloy involved brains. I don't think these did, but they were a deliciously smoked sausage. There are modern products that use the name but have none of the taste or smell. The saveloy shop, Darby's if I remember correctly, had a queue well down the high street. (My mother, an obsessively law-abiding soul, once received a ticket for causing an obstruction: she had parked near Darby's for fear they would run out and father would be upset.) You could eat stewed eels in Ramsgate. Back home in Broadstairs the man with the wooden barrow came every Sunday selling 'humps', a variety of shrimp. So many places sold crabs, whelks and cockles that it was not where you could get them but who sold the best. We always had teal, widgeon, woodcock, snipe and hares (in season) hanging in the cellar near the wooden barrel of beer delivered by the local brewery.

## IN A SENSE THERE'S BEEN NO REVOLUTION: SAME OLD BAD TRAITS

It is possible to argue that the revolution has been for better or for worse. It is equally possible to argue that there has been no revolution at all. That beef in wine dish so scorned in 1963 is just as scorned today, but for different reasons. Then it was strange; now it is not new enough. Every week, newspapers, magazines and TV programmes unveil new dishes, and restaurants and chefs announce new culinary creations, new menus – even new cuisines. Each of these means bypassing something that was old, tried, excellent and classic; and all for the sake of novelty. The beef in wine is not new enough and it is too simple. How can you put a signature on it?

Even if modern England had the range of ingredients for good cooking, they would be inadequate to make up a good national diet. The key questions are: how good are the ingredients and what is done with them? How suitable are they for good dishes? How do we cook, serve and eat them? If you want to know whether food in England has really improved over the last 30 or 40 years you should avert your eyes from the massed ranks of colourful vegetables and fruit at the greengrocer's and the well-dressed slab of fish at the – increasingly difficult to find – fishmonger's, and instead examine in detail what happens to just one or two of the products. First, there are several of these new foods that are seldom bought and cooked by English people. Aubergines are a case in point. Many others that are bought a little more often are purchased in minuscule quantities, demonstrating that they are destined for use in dishes very different from those common in France or Italy. You will still hear that quiet bleating in the greengrocer's: 'I'd like *a* pepper, please.' You can't make *piperade* with *a* green pepper!

This tendency to go for minuscule amounts is but a continuation of an old practice: England is the only country in which I have ever seen pre-cut quarters of cucumbers for sale. The explanation is the same as for 'a' green pepper. The shopper is not going to make a dish with cucumber or peppers. She has no idea of the large number of good dishes she could make with either. She just wants a bit to go in a mixed salad or to garnish, say, a cold poached salmon. All those new sorts of fungi on sale – hardly anyone buys sufficient of them to make a dish of them. They are to sit on top of the veal escalope to justify calling it something other than a Waitrose veal escalope. The Korean at the market buys three huge Chinese cabbages: she is going to make *kimchee* to eat over the coming weeks or months. Her Italian cousin buys five pounds of peppers, five of aubergines and a pound of garlic: she is going to dunk them in boiling wine vinegar and make a pickle in oil for use at several *antipasti*. Their English cousin wants one aubergine – she is worried because they absorb a lot of oil and that's not healthy. She wants one pepper, for a garnish, and she asks, 'Is it possible to buy half a Chinese cabbage? One's too much.' If you list these token purchases – aubergines, tinda, chillies, Chinese cabbage, etc. – and subtract them from the revolutionary agenda, things rapidly look decidedly less colourful, new and diverse. And novelty and colour almost disappear when we look at the 'new' foods that have been rather more generously embraced. Let us consider in the next chapter those naughty old ways that ruin good food.

CHAPTER 2

DROWNING IN CULINARY INCOMPETENCE

### NO REVOLUTION: OLD WAYS WITH NEW FOODS

The first English reaction to courgettes that I can remember was from a neighbour who spotted some growing in my garden. I lived in Derbyshire at the time. She looked suspicious. 'We call them "coojettes"', she said. It turned out that neither she nor her friends ate them, nor did they grow them. If I wanted proper vegetables, she explained, I should go to the such-and-such where they did a wonderful roast Sunday dinner with eight vegetables – none of them 'coojettes'. I never did work out why the courgette had been singled out for renaming, whether it was a sign of derision, and who the 'we' were that had conspired to rename them. The only possibly salient information I can offer about her taste and judgement was that asparagus grew prolifically in her garden and she didn't eat that either. Indeed, she said it was a weed, dug it up and burnt it. This was in 1978, more than a quarter of a century ago, but well into the supposed revolutionary era.

### BOILING VEGETABLES: THE LOVE AFFAIR
### WITH WATER AND SIZE

Courgettes arrived in England at the end of the sixties – about 10 years before my northern neighbour re-christened them. Before that you could get them at specialist markets such as Berwick Street in London, but they were not known in restaurants, on domestic dinner tables or in gardens throughout most of the country. Courgettes are a good, if humble, example of what really happened during the revolution. Once upon a time nobody had them. Now, after an initial dismissive reaction, everyone has them. And pretty horrid they are, too. 'Courgette' is a French word which means a little marrow. In theory, courgettes are a great improvement on marrows. The English knew about marrows before the David 'revolution'. Men grew them on allotments and took pride in their size. In England, size was then a valued quality in many things, including leeks (the French have always mystified the English by favouring thin, young leeks). Turnips, too, are prized for their size here, while the perverse French like tiny spring turnips: how can you win a competition with tiny turnips? The English liked – and many of them still do like – big parsnips, swedes and runner beans. The longer, tougher and stringier the better.

The pre-David English had ways of dealing with these enormous vegetables. They boiled them to make them soft. They loved watery veg anyway, so marrows, which are mostly water, were appreciated. However, first they sensibly removed the pith and pips from the middle. Then they boiled chunks of marrow, and on festive occasions served them in lumpy white sauce made with corn flour. More accomplished cooks stuffed them whole, but de-pithed, with minced meat. They were edible even in the scorching heatwaves of the English summer – refreshing, as water tends to be.

The first courgettes were imported. They came from countries where the people were used to eating courgettes; countries that had highly developed food cultures, mostly Latin and olive-oil based. The vegetables were, as they should be, less than two inches long and were the diameter of a finger. Because they were young, they had next to no pips or pith. You sliced them and made *beignets* of them or used them in a *ratatouille*. The *ratatouille*'s other stronger ingredients of tomatoes, peppers and aubergines ensured no one could get bored with the courgettes. As the English started to grow courgettes for themselves, commercially and in their gardens, the native giganticist and hydrophiliac tendencies reasserted themselves. Courgettes got longer, fatter, pithier and pippier. But since the Latin recipes did not command the pith to be removed, it was not removed, and the courgette, with pith and pips, turned out to be a worse vegetable than the properly treated marrow ever was. You see, there had been no revolution: the national predilections for size and water were unreformed.

## THE ENGLISH FONDNESS FOR FIVE BAD VEGETABLES RATHER THAN ONE GOOD ONE

And so it was with another national tendency. The pre-David marrow, once prepared and boiled, would be served with, say, roast lamb, roast potatoes, boiled potatoes (preferably floury and disintegrating), carrots and peas, mint sauce with sugar, gravy, stale powdered white pepper and salt sprinkled from a Bakelite salt cellar (the hole of which had to be cleared at each mealtime, having become clogged with salt sodden by the steam from the kitchen in which the five vegetables were being furiously boiled). Traditionally, the English loved meat with five or more vegetables. Indeed, as noted above, I have heard restaurants rated solely by the number of vegetables they served, with quality totally ignored.

In French cooking, meat is traditionally accompanied by a token vegetable, a sort of garnish; for instance, a blood pudding might have one *pomme vapeur*. To some extent, bread plays the role that a starch vegetable such as the ubiquitous potato plays in England. Sometimes a dish might call for one particular vegetable with meat, as in a *cassoulet* of various meats with white beans, or grilled lamb with *flageolets*, or pickled cabbage with pork and sausages in *choucroute*. Even in stewed beef and veal dishes that call for, say, carrots, one uses the carrots sparingly. And the first batch, having flavoured the stock, are thrown out and replaced by a few more. Otherwise, vegetables, especially composed vegetable dishes, can be a course on their own before, or more likely after, the meat. Certainly the French, who eat fish much more often than the English, would never load a fish dish with accompanying vegetables.

This has never been understood in England; or if it has, it has been steadfastly resisted. Both before and after the supposed revolution, in a majority of today's English restaurants, what happens is this. You have pork in sauce X and your friend has duck in sauce Y. At the next table, the couple want, respectively, a sole and *cannelloni*. Regardless of what the main ingredient is, you are all offered the same selection of *ratatouille*, *petits pois*, spinach, mashed potatoes and fennel in lemon sauce. At domestic tables these might even be put out already on the diners' plates. In restaurants, the vegetables are served in individual personal ashtrays. It is an insult not only to the meat and fish, but also to the spurned composed vegetable dishes. Some diners make it worse by mixing all this up in an unharmonious mess on their plates. But the point is that nothing, but nothing has changed. The English are taking their vegetables as they always have done – promiscuously, excessively and without taste. Presumably, given all the warring flavours and textures that result, they don't notice the pith and the pips of the courgette.

What the courgette saga shows is that you cannot improve a national cuisine just by bringing in new foods. The key issue is what English people do to courgettes and the other new foods. If they continue with their size obsession (which is really a form of meanness), if they persist in the promiscuous variety of vegetables, if they continue to delight in wateriness rather than taste, then, although the food will be different, it will be no better.

And there is one further cultural tendency exemplified by the humble courgette. English holiday-makers abroad will have observed the way good cooking cultures take a delight in the bounties of nature and respond to any food opportunity with alacrity and also with effort. See, for instance, the French or Spanish scouring the countryside for snails or mushrooms after rain. Here, no one bothers, though our snails are of the same – Roman – type. The courgette may itself be dull, but it has a delicious appendage, which fetches high prices among the cultures that know it. This is its flower. Large yellow courgette flowers, blanched and stuffed with minced pork and herbs or crab meat and gently heated, form a dish up there with the greats. As I write, it is the season – August. I can see courgette flowers decomposing in so many gardens. No one wants them. No one can be bothered. They prefer pith, pips and water.

## THE ENGLISH AND TOMATOES

The incompetent treatment of courgettes does not, in fact, ruin many dishes: just the courgettes themselves and any meat or fish dish they are served with. For an example of something treated incompetently that does wreck many dishes, look no further than the tomato. Before the alleged revolution, tomatoes eaten in England were grown in this country or were imported from Spain and the Canaries. The home-grown ones were alright for the occasional primitive salad and their taste was anyway masked by the all-powerful malt vinegar and salad cream that were *de rigueur* in the pre-revolutionary age. They were refreshing in a curious way. The tomatoes were fine for frying with eggs and bacon. And these were the uses to which they were put. But the tomato today is used with pasta, in sauces and a whole range of dishes. Its potential for sabotage is far greater.

Tomatoes consist of tomato flesh and juice, skin, water, pith and pips. What is needed for fine food are the flesh and the juice. What the tomatoes themselves need are good soil to give flavour and sun to ripen the fruit quickly. And where do modern Britons buy their tomatoes? From Holland – a place with little soil, less sun, but an addiction to water that rivals

England's. Take a Dutch tomato, skin it, cut it in half, add salt to the flesh and leave it for 30 minutes. Pour out the water, scrape out the pips and cut out the whitish pith. There will be next to no flesh left. It is not really a tomato at all. It is like a piece of steak that is all fat, gristle and plastic wrapping with no lean flesh. Last July, I went to a selection of local greengrocers. July is a month when sunny countries with good soil – the South of France, Italy and Spain – are full of excellent tomatoes. The only ones in the shops were Dutch and tasteless. There were five different sorts: plum, beef, ordinary, cherry and vine, but all Dutch. As one greengrocer explained, 'these are what people want; they present well'. Some revolution.

These apparently various but all-the-same tomatoes from Holland are not inflicted on the consumer by the greengrocers or the supermarkets as some lefty food writers allege (it is interesting how food writers often are lefties but that explains why they so often blame suppliers and are soft on the consuming masses). It is the mass consumer who inflicts them on cooks and eaters of discretion because the mass consumer won't buy anything else: 'They look nice.'

### THE ENGLISH AND SALMON

Rather different examples of change and continuity in eating and cooking can be seen in the case of ingredients such as salmon, hens, bacon joints, brains, game, bread and rice. Salmon used to be expensive and a high-quality fish because it was wild. It is now cheap, farmed and often of inferior quality. As far as I can see, the English have failed to notice the difference in quality at all. They cook and eat salmon in their homes much as they always have, grilled in steaks (it is true they occasionally change the names of dishes; these were, for a time, called *darnes*) or poached and served hot or cold. In truth, the fish was never poached, but was boiled and overdone. Sometimes, cooked in a steamer, the bottom half of the fish used to be overdone, while the top half was raw! In the early seventies it was poached in foil, but was even more overdone since no one could see when it was ready. Sometimes the salmon was served with fake hollandaise, sometimes with slices of cucumber (from that quarter?) in malt vinegar. Both effectively obliterated any taste that remained after the over-boiling, but to be on the safe side diners were offered bottled *ersatz* mayonnaise. Frozen peas and new potatoes were (and still are) also served.

This abomination continues more or less unchanged. It has not been subjected to even the gentlest revolution. One *could* argue that there has been a change for the better: today we ruin flavourless, cheap, farmed salmon, whereas we used to ruin flavourful, expensive wild salmon. But there has also been a change for the worse: since salmon is now, mackerel and herring aside, the cheapest well-known fish available, the abomination is produced and inflicted on dinner guests far more frequently.

There are, in fact, all sorts of good dishes that can be made from cheap farmed salmon, but they all require some effort. For example, the fish can be skinned, filleted, salted and cured in oil with chillies, or in lemon. But the English cannot be bothered. Restaurants have recognized the cheapness of salmon and put it in fishcakes. It makes some of the driest fishcakes imaginable. Other cheap fish, such as gurnard or skate knobs make much better cakes, but these are rarely used. No doubt the restaurateurs know the English would be frightened by the unfamiliar. What we see in the case of salmon is a sort of pig-headed ritualism. The fish has changed but, since it has the same name, we shall go on doing what we always did to it – which was pretty unpleasant anyway.

## THE ENGLISH AND CHICKENS

Hens, and by that I mean old boiling hens, are another interesting case. They used to be readily available from street markets and butchers but are now more difficult to get. The sole remaining source seems to be halal shops. They were essential for that splendid old English dish of boiled chicken, with carrots, onions, possibly pearl barley, and parsley sauce. They were also good for French chicken stews like Provencal *daubes* and, of course, for long, slow-cooking curries. With their more or less total departure, we have lost several first-rate dishes. Also gone are boiling bacon joints – or rather, they are not gone but they are no longer any good. Brains have gone, banned by interfering governments, and so have sweetbreads. For Bertie Wooster, Anatole's sweetbreads *à la financière* were the best dish imaginable. And he was following in a solid French tradition. In the case of hens, brains, sweetbreads and bacon, there has been a revolution alright, but it is one for the worse.

## GAME THAT NO ONE WANTS EXCEPT 'FOR A CHANGE'

Game and other wild meats, such as rabbit, are still available. The English are some of the luckiest people in the world because they have an abundance of pheasants, hares, partridges, pigeons, rabbit and wild duck at very low prices. The prices are low because no one wants game, especially if they have to hang, pluck or skin it themselves. Every year when the game season starts, a food journalist will write a column suggesting people try a pheasant or partridge 'for a change'. A few readers will dutifully obey and subsequently announce to their friends that 'it made a nice change'. What is this 'change' business? Why not eat hare this week, partridge next week, mallard after that, then rabbit, then teal, then wild goose, then pheasant, then hare *pâté*, then widgeon, then pheasant sausages, then rabbit terrine, then the whole list again from September to the end of January? Who, in his right mind, wants a change from this? But the extraordinarily ungrateful, lazy, nervous attitude to game does not change at all.

## BREAD

Bread has already been mentioned. What needs emphasizing is that the key question is not whether bread has got worse or better over the past forty years. It is that the English, at least those of them who think they have adapted to a more Latin, less traditional English, style of food, still don't understand what to do with bread. The reason why fish and meat in sauces can be served without vegetables in France or Spain is that the bread acts as a vegetable, and indeed as a pusher, just as it does in northern Indian and Pakistani food. It is not there to be spread with butter. And whether bread is good comes down to whether it is the sort of bread that is good for pulling, soaking and pushing. Obviously sliced bread and those 1970s exploding, air-filled rolls are no use at all. But, equally obviously, those restaurants that today serve bread in ten varieties, covered in various seeds and stuffed with different nonsenses, all in a large basket and selected with the aid of tongs have also missed the point. The bread is to accompany a flavour, not to replace it.

## RICE

The story of the fate of rice is similarly revealing. Forty years ago there were two sorts of rice available: pudding rice and long-grain Patna. Now there is Italian Arborio, Spanish rice, Indian basmati, perfumed Thai, Chinese glutinous rice and several more. Of course this is an improvement. But whether it has an improving effect on the kitchen and table is quite another matter. My experience is that the English are still fearful of rice and are inclined to cook it for too long and with too much water or, more rarely, too briefly and with too little water. This is probably because they have too little practice. One regularly overhears conversations in which someone is praising this brand of rice or that type of rice steamer because it works so well and makes this difficult task of rice cooking trouble free. The truth is that basic rice cooking can be done in any old container if the cook is prepared to practise and, with rices such as basmati, prepared to wash the rice enough times.

## THE LOSS OF STOCKS AND FATS

With Arborio risotto and some Spanish dishes, what usually goes wrong is that the cook has no meat or fish stock of adequate quality; perhaps no stock at all. Their mothers would have had at least meat and chicken stocks. The pre-David generation used to have a regular supply of home-made stocks, and that is why, when, on the rare, festive occasions that they got round to it, they could makes good soups and sauces – and why so many contemporary cooks can't. While we are at it, the same point applies to fats. That old generation also kept a supply of home-rendered fats, usually in distressed tea-cups – beef, pork and, unfortunately, lamb. These fats have today been replaced – occasionally by good olive oil, but more often by boring polyunsaturates, some of which have boiling points too low for the task in hand, hence those frequently soggy chips.

The lesson to be drawn from rice is that practice and effort bring improvement; it does not all depend on the variety of ingredient. The lesson from stocks and fats is rather different: good cooking depends on maintaining a good kitchen with good supplies, and this means daily maintenance. It is simply not possible to desert the kitchen for 13 days, then invite some chums to dinner on Saturday and imagine an hour's shopping will supply all that is needed. Good food requires cooking and shopping every day. Indeed, the older generation of Spanish and French would say shopping ought to be done twice a day.

It is readily obvious from the overloaded trolleys in any supermarket, and indeed from the overloaded bags leaving most butchers, that the English do not shop daily. Studies of family eating patterns show they do not eat together daily either.

Judged by the criteria of hard work, daily effort in the kitchen and high street, conscientious practice in the kitchen, and the maintenance of a good larder, there has indeed been a revolution, but again it has been for the worse.

## THE LOSS OF BREAKFAST: A THEME THAT RECURS THROUGHOUT THESE PAGES

There is more bad news. Not only have some new ingredients had their impact blunted, distorted or reversed by incompetent cooking practices and attitudes, but whole meals have been subverted. Tea has more or less disappeared and, much more serious, breakfast has been destroyed. Foreigners always used to say they could put up with ghastly English food because at least the breakfasts were good. But this national institution has collapsed. Why and how?

The minimum English breakfast is bacon, eggs and toast. That requires free-range fairly fresh eggs, bacon that is not injected with water, and bread thick enough to toast and firm enough to mop up the delicious fat from the fried eggs without disintegrating.

The more elaborate breakfast could include kidneys (which must not have been frozen or they will steam and harden, rather than fry); sausages, which should be largely fresh pork with some fat (but only enough to moisten them) and genuine intestine skins; and fresh, field mushrooms, bread or potatoes fried in pork or bacon fat, and freshly mixed mustard.

Variants on the breakfast theme would include poached haddock and poached eggs, home-made baked beans and bubble and squeak, boiled duck eggs with soldiers, and kippers.

All these ingredients are still available, but it takes hard work to find them. It also requires hard work to make your own sausages, when necessary, and baked beans and bubble and squeak. Simply, those responsible for food in most English families are not prepared to do the work. This hardly matters, because it would seem those for whom these breakfasts might be made are too lazy to get up and eat them properly round a table. They are even too lazy to eat them out. There has been a massive decline in the number of transport cafés serving traditional breakfasts, at least at breakfast time. So lazy is the nation that a new sign has emerged announcing 'Breakfasts all day'.

When one does eat a breakfast out, there is one overriding problem with it (quite apart from eggs so stale they spread across the plate, oversalted bacon that has steamed and that yields peculiar orange deposits, fried bread as thin as a crisp and industrial 'hash-browns'). The worst thing about it is that it is sitting in a great puddle of water that has seeped from tinned mushrooms and that mixes all the tastes up. Hydrophilia again. The loss of the English breakfast will be referred to again and again in this book, partly because there is no excuse for it. It was so easy to do and so good to eat. Its rejection is a national disgrace.

# CHAPTER 3

# THE TENDENCIES THAT RUIN ENGLISH FOOD

In chapters one and two we saw that some aspects of English food have changed but by no means always for the better. We also saw that, in some important ways, there has been little change. What is it that makes our meals so bad? There are *nine* tendencies. I want to consider eight of them now, reserving one for sustained attention in chapter 5. I start with a couple we have encountered already.

## THE LOVE OF WATER

I must emphasize that the tendencies are just that, tendencies. They are not principles. One might, I suppose have some perverted respect for a nation that only and always ate food drowned in water. The English are not like that. The predilection for the water breaks out in one dish, but then is forgotten or even contradicted in another. Nevertheless it is an important tendency, contributing to some spectacular culinary disasters. As we have already seen, the English enthusiastically buy watery, tasteless Dutch tomatoes and pithy, oversized tasteless courgettes. Whole sections of the vegetable counter are now given over to produce from Holland, a land that has never got over its own watery origins. Perhaps love of water is the wrong way to describe this tendency. You could also call it a love of the tasteless, the bland and the insipid, and a concomitant dislike, or even fear, of strong tastes. But water is often involved. Go to any middle-class English house for dinner. After dinner – good or bad, but usually terrible – the hostess

will chirp, 'Who's for coffee?' Silly question. Everyone of any taste wants coffee after dinner. A well-run French house would just serve it, no questions asked. But, no, three of us refuse, offering the feeble and palpably untrue excuse, 'I can't, I'm afraid.' (Well, I suppose the 'afraid' part is true. Fancy a grown man trembling at the prospect of a tiny cup of coffee!) Next we are asked, 'How do you take it?' The obvious answer is: 'Strong and black, of course, why do you ask?' But no, again. Two guests are ill-bred enough to want to dilute it with milk. Another wants it *sans* coffee, that is decaffeinated, and only two want it as it is. 'As it is' turns out to be with gallons of water. I suspect the hostess would really like to serve it in huge mugs bearing unfunny slogans, so that yet more water could be introduced. As the guests sip their dishwater, she reassures them, 'There's plenty more in the pot.'

She has at least prepared them earlier in the dinner for this, its watery end. They started with a seafood salad, squid on mixed salad leaves. The squid had been frozen. It was Californian. For some reason Californian frozen squid exudes water when it is cooked, so it doesn't fry, but rather boils and goes hard. Water again. The salad leaves had been washed but not dried, and the wet leaves won't coat with *vinaigrette*. All this was followed by gammon, thoughtfully injected with water by its processors, and now served on rice that has been overcooked in too much water. The whole show was preceded by gin and tonics. These were made by taking a warm glass, adding warm gin and ice cubes and warm tonic. Not unnaturally, the ice instantly melts, making the gin and tonic flat – and watery.

English food of the fifties was saturated in water. Vegetables were overcooked in it, and then gallons more water were poured over it under the alias of 'gravy'. Gravy is seldom mentioned now, but the old hydrophilia remains. One of its new incarnations is as 'light' foods. There is light (or 'lite') beer, light olive oil, light cigarettes, light bread, light biscuits, light cooking oil. I once saw a sausage labelled 'light'. What 'light' means, of course, is tasteless, weak, insipid. I suppose it reflects the wider mania for water. People keep sucking away on bottles of it all day in public, like children at a teat. They are always in the bathroom; 'bathrooms', I should say, since modern houses seem to consist of nothing else. Even food cranks such as vegetarians conform. They seem to choose watery vegetarian dishes, sloppy pink boring lentils, over-cooked mushy cauliflowers, stodgy, damp bread, insipid quich-es. And water can even ruin what remains of the glory of an English breakfast. What happens is that bacon, eggs and sausages are fried and served with fried bread. As I mentioned above, at the last moment a tin of mushrooms, heated in their own water, is poured onto the plate. Even if they are drained, which they usually are not, they ooze grey and horrid-tasting water into everything, producing soggy fried bread and obscuring the taste of the eggs.

## SQUEAMISHNESS, FASTIDIOUSNESS AND THE FEAR OF SMELLS AND BONES

The list of ingredients and dishes that are highly valued by the best cuisines in the world – French, Chinese, Italian, Spanish, Indian – but rejected by the English, is a long one. We shall return to it in the chapters on shopping and on rejecting food. But here and now we might mention:

brains

anchovies

strong goat's cheese

(I don't mean that boring lemony-tasting nothing made by Goodlifers in the West Country)

tripe, especially *andouillette*

(I read that J. K. Rowling, an important figure in the world of modern children, has named tripe her least favourite food; *Daily Telegraph*, 10 January 2006.)

eels

whelks

sea snails

pigs' ears

well-hung game

small bony fish

karela (or bitter gourd)

testicles (bulls', rams' and hogs')

dandelion leaves

blood

cephalopods

pig and ox liver

fish heads

and anything that wobbles in aspic

That'll do for the moment. Anchovies and goat's cheese are simply too strong for the effete modern Briton. The anchovies, karela and the dandelion are too bitter. The bony fish require controlled use of a knife and fork and intelligent mastication, and that is too much of an effort. With the *andouillette*, tripe and pigs' ears the rejection is more psychological (read sentimental), and it is especially the smell of tripe and *andouillette* that appears to arouse the aversion. Similarly the texture of jelly seems to frighten Albion to death. Some of the English don't think food has any business smelling of anything. They complain if a restaurant or pub smells of food. (As an aside and a matter for someone else to explain, these same people themselves smell revolting. They are forever spraying themselves with cheap scent or powdering themselves with talc after their frequent and unnecessary showers). Genuine lovers of food love the smell of it. And note, too, many English people don't like the look of food, either – especially the raw ingredients. Me, I'll stand happily in the queue at the butcher's; indeed, I prefer it when there is a queue so that I can gaze at that fore-quarter of beef hanging beyond the open door of the cold storage. If they rented deckchairs in the *Boqueria* market in Barcelona, I'd willingly pay to sit and gaze at the blood puddings for half an hour. The English especially dislike the sight of cooked food if it resembles the principal raw ingredient. While the Edwardians would go to extreme lengths to craft bits of fish and meat to look like a fish or animal, modern Britons like their chicken surrounded by, covered in, or otherwise disguised by anything, just so they are not reminded of its origins. There is a vogue now among professional people and bureaucrats to insist on the 'traceability' of food. But the problem is not that there are too few certificates and regulations. It is that English culture does not want to know – is horrified by – the actual origins of food.

Good cooks like the feel of food. Dough is a favourite (and it is wonderful for cleaning your nails). Or there's the deep pleasure at that moment when your hand has felt its way up a fat duck's bottom, finally clasps the stomach, loosens it and pulls it away; or when it cracks a rabbit's jaw to test that the animal is young enough to fry. Add it up. They don't like the smell of food, the sight of food, the taste of tasty food. They don't like food. The English go to enormous lengths in their rejection of these things they are afraid of. Obviously they don't buy them. But when they are offered them, they make faces and say 'urgh' or 'oh'. If they find an offensive item on their plate they smuggle it onto the rim and hide it under a piece of bread. They pretend they aren't hungry or claim one of the more fashionable allergies: anything to avoid actually eating the anchovy or pig's ear. The most pathetic excuse is a simpering smile and an apparently self-deprecating, 'Sorry, I never could eat liver; it's memories of school food; it's silly of me, I suppose.' It is true that the liver at the best schools was always rotten, but so was chapel religion and the teaching of Trollope. That does not mean sensible adults keep up self-denying vendettas on religion and great literature for the rest of their days.

Whatever the excuse, the English leave an enormous amount of food on their plates. At a dinner party in France all the plates will be clean. In England two-thirds will have something substantial left on them. Some is left because of fear of taste, the effort of manipulation or mastication, infantile habits, texture, colour or whatever. Some is left because the diner has taken too much. The diners actually say, 'I can't eat any more, it was delicious.' Then why did they take it? These people are so out of touch with their tummies they cannot gauge their own appetites.

## SPECIAL OCCASIONISM

In the fifties only middle-class people went out to restaurants – I mean restaurants, not tearooms or cafés. They went for special occasions or 'treats'. It might be someone's birthday or anniversary, a holiday, or an act of generosity to guests staying in the home. I recall they started with varieties of 'cream' soups: cream of asparagus, cream of chicken and, of course, cream of tomato. There was grapefruit, cut in half with a bottled glacé cherry in the middle and brown sugar sprinkled over the top. On the rare occasions that *pâté* appeared, it was accompanied by thin 'Melba' toast sweating in a table napkin. If there was melon, it was accompanied by stale powdered ginger. The *tour de force* was an hors d'oeuvres trolley with revolving layers of dishes. They contained tinned sardines, pickled silverskin onions, red cabbage, cold baked beans, potato salad in salad cream, *macédoine* of tinned vegetables – a distant cousin of sandwich spread or 'sick' as we young people called it – and Danish salami.

Once on the plate, the deep red vinegar from the red cabbage mixed and curdled with the salad cream and tomato sauce. For a main course there were roasts, steak, duck and sole, all served with lots of vegetables but no bread. The high spot was the pudding, which was even more garish than the hors d'oeuvres. In truth, the main courses were not bad. They were, at least, not pretentious. But any of them could have been cooked at home. For the point of going out was not to have special food but to 'go out', to have an occasion, to dine by the light of a candle in a Blue Nun bottle. The food did not matter.

Today, of course, the English dine out much more frequently. While no one could say that eating out is a special occasion, the English are still obsessed with the non-food trappings of restaurants. Two food writers who know their business, A. A. Gill and Jonathan Meades, and one I am less persuaded by, Giles Coren, feel obliged to postpone discussion of food till about half-way through their columns. Clearly the English don't want too many words wasted on the actual food. What they get – and presumably want – is a lot of words on the place, what it looks like, the sort of people who go there. Anything but the food. This is a vestige of Special Occasionism. But to see SO in its full glory you have to look at eating in the home. Again, in the fifties, the average mother cooked twenty-three family meals a week: breakfast, lunch and supper every day, with tea at the weekends. Now, as we have seen, it is not just breakfast that is a rarity; any properly cooked and eaten family meal is a special occasion. Indeed, there are households where the only time a full meal is cooked from raw is when guests come for a dinner party. It should be obvious that one cannot cook well like this. It is expensive because one has to start from scratch every time. The spices, herbs, fats and stocks, which in a well-run home should be renewed regularly, have to be bought *en bloc*, and there is a lot left over that will not keep to the next special occasion. But even more importantly, good cooking demands practice. Even simple dishes such as steamed rice or a Spanish omelette require practice: practice in finding out which rice or what sorts of potatoes work and where to find them, and practice in cooking them.

Practice entails repetition, and Special Occasionism rules repetition out. Routine is just as important. A task such as making bread requires practice. But once learned it does not take up much time, provided it is established as part of a daily routine. So, it takes a few seconds to start the yeast going; the flour is added a few minutes later; and then the bread is made some hours later. But it has to be incorporated in the day, every day.

Because Special Occasionists only cook and entertain every couple of weeks or so, they turn dinner, which to any sensible cook and eater is a routine, businesslike affair, into a Gala. Guests have to eat flanked by four knives, three forks, a line of glasses and a galaxy of coasters, candles, table decorations, flowers and bunting. Wilde's dictum about being overdressed applies as much to dinner tables as to people. Occasionists plot: 'If we're going to have Nigel, we must have Jackie, and I've always wanted to see how Peter and Geoffrey will get on; they're so opposite, wouldn't it be fun...' Special Occasionists divide ingredients and dishes into two groups: ordinary ones and treats. It's treats that get served at dinner parties. So you never get given an ordinary French beef stew or some fried kidneys or salt pork. Treats have to be special. That means they have to cost a lot; or, more accurately, be perceived to have cost a lot. Since the relative price of food changes, the treat business throws up odd choices. Asparagus has only risen threefold in price during a period when salaries have risen more than tenfold and food in general less than tenfold. Asparagus is now cheap. But it is still regarded as a treat and thus fit for the dinner party. Cuttlefish, which used to be more or less free, is now comparatively expensive but is not a 'treat'. Pheasants are now extremely cheap: I pay less for one than for a half pint of beer, but they are still a treat. You know they are a treat because when anyone serves one, a guest will obligingly coo, 'Oooh, pheasant, what a treat!' One great danger of the treat nonsense occurs when a dish is served that has two varieties, such as farmed and wild salmon. Here it is up to the hostess to help us recognize that the dish awaiting us is of the treat variety. She says, 'I managed to get some wild salmon.' Then we can all coo, 'What a treat!'

Treat status can also be influenced by fashion, perceived rarity, perceived difficulty in creation – or simply by being served in minuscule portions. From the point of view of good food, the treat/ordinary division results in the narrowing of dinner-party menus to the point where we dare not go out for fear of being offered sea bass for the third time in two weeks. It also affects daily ordinary eating, since 'treats' are not allowed. The only way to get to eat a wild duck is to have eight people to dinner. This explains the question I posed in an earlier chapter about why food columnists produce the bizarre sentence at the beginning of the game season: 'Why not try a pheasant/mallard/partridge for a change?' Any sensible family will eat these regularly, but the Special Occasionists cannot for they are treats, reserved for special occasions. It would be a revolution indeed to eat them on your own on a Wednesday.

### MEANNESS

I also said the English were mean about food, but I am not sure 'mean' is quite the right term. In the last decade of the twentieth century, that is, well after the so-called 'food revolution', the average family was spending 17 per cent of its income on food. As they have become more affluent, they have come to spend proportionately less on food: a decade earlier they were spending 30 per cent. A decade before that, in other words before the 'great food revolution', the lower classes were spending up to half their incomes on food. It is now below a quarter. As all classes get more money, they obviously have a choice of what to spend it on. The Family Expenditure Survey, which produced these figures, explains what people are buying with their new wealth. It is not calf liver and red mullet, but shell suits and funerals for pets. That tells you all you need to know about contemporary food culture. Moreover, the sums spent on food are consistently lower than those spent by the French, Italians and Spanish.

Surveys of spending by the poorest classes in England also show there is a huge variation, with some families spending double what others do to feed the same number of people. So the basic data suggest that we spend as little as we can on domestic food, and the policy talk reinforces this with its constant references to the 'cheap food policy' that so annoys the Greens. There are other indications of meanness. Go to any of the few remaining street or covered markets and find yourself a line of greengrocer stalls. Read the notices and listen to the sales talk. This one is offering onions at ten pence cheaper than that; this one's tomatoes are five pence cheaper than at the neighbouring stall. The shoppers crowd around looking to see; to see what? The prices. The competition is not for the best, the firmest, the best dried, the sweetest or the mildest onions, but for the cheapest. Nearly all the information given is about price. You will even hear shoppers bragging to their friends, 'How much did you pay for your onions, 20p? I got mine for 18p.' Who cares about quality?

Then go to the high street for a couple of other examples of meanness. The first is in the butcher's (Friday and Saturday are the days for this). A lady approaches the counter: 'I'd like a joint of beef please.' 'Yes, Madam, a nice piece of topside, or sirloin or...' He stops. Her eyes have glazed over. 'You find me a nice one', she says. 'About how much?' he asks. 'Eight pounds.' 'Eight pounds weight or eight pounds money?' 'Eight pounds money.' What she is saying is that she neither knows nor cares about the type of joint. She does not even care about whether it will be enough to feed her family or guests. Anything will do that fits the price.

The second example concerns the whole high street. There is much talk today about the high street being in decline. Small shops are being forced to close by the heavy-handed competition of the out-of-town supermarkets. The supposition is that the supermarkets are undercutting the high street on price and are more convenient for parking. The first is not always the case. I have always found supermarkets more expensive than high streets for meat and fish, and far more expensive for everything than street markets except tinned and packaged goods. But the point is this: the supermarkets do not force the high-street shops out of business. No one forces the customer to desert the small shop and drive to the supermarket. The customer freely chooses to do this. He, or she, does this because he saves, overall, a few pence – say 5 per cent of his 17 per cent of income spent on food; less than 1 per cent of his total income. The customer is so mean that he will wreck his local high street to save less than 1 per cent of his income. He probably does not save that when the petrol he uses to get to and from the supermarket is factored in. But then he is not only mean; he is lazy.

It is, as I say, an odd meanness. The measures of how much is spent on food are fairly accurate and reliable. In contrast, little formal data exist on how much food is wasted. We know some food is never served. It stays in the larder or fridge and goes off. Still more is left on the sides of plates or serving dishes, especially by children. How odd that the same people who are mean about food should waste it. But they do. The only way I can reconcile the two is to say these people care little about food. They do not consider it worthy of a substantial proportion of their income, and they do not believe it matters if it is thrown away. That would fit in with another characteristic, which is that they seldom enthuse articulately about food either in shops or while eating.

## LAZINESS

Every so often someone sounds off about the need to liberate ladies from household chores. Another phrase is to unshackle the modern woman from the cooker. Ladies are 'slaves to the stove'. Women's magazines are full of hints to make the chores easier. Jane Clarke writing in *The Times* (19 November 2005) recommends lentils. She explains that 'one of the reasons I love lentils is that unlike other pulses there is no need to soak them before cooking'. Now, we should remember that it is these 'other pulses' themselves that have to do the long soaking – not the cook herself. All the cook has to do is to remember to pour them into water at the right time, a matter of ten seconds. Apparently so daunting is this task that any pulse (such as the lentil) that offers a release from it is to be embraced. Someone else writes a regular column in *The Times* on quick and easy cooking. Women's magazines have a regular theme running through them, which is how to 'cheat' at cooking. This is usually not a hint on how to pass off something cheap as a more expensive ingredient or dish, but rather on how to look as if you have made an effort when you have not.

It is common knowledge that modern families cannot be bothered to eat together at the dinner table – or even at the kitchen table. A survey by Cranks, reported in *The Times* (4 June 2005), revealed that one family in four does not even *possess* a dinner or kitchen table. Even among the three-quarters that do own a table, only a fifth use it for eating off. Instead it is used for hobbies or as a centrepiece to look at. If one member of the family should have the apparently perverted inclination to eat with another, this is now accomplished side by side on the sofa. This was uncovered in a study by sociologist Esther Dermott, who reported that eating meals together 'did not come up as something that was important to [fathers] at all... They picked out activity-based things like football or going to the school play. These were the times they talked to kids. The idea of sitting around a table has disappeared' (*Daily Telegraph*, 4 June 2005). Of course, one attraction of the sofa is that it is where the members of the family were seated before eating and it is where they will be seated after eating. So not only can the mother not be bothered to cook properly and the family not be bothered to eat properly

together, but by dint of eating on the sofa no one need make the effort to move the ten feet from sofa to table and back again.

What they eat on their sofas is mostly snacks or part meals. Increasingly even these are not prepared at home but bought chilled from a supermarket and microwaved at home. The chilled food market is now worth £1 billion. Those who report this unsavoury state of affairs are quick to point out that they in no way blame the family, let alone the mother. It arises because all the family members are rushed off their feet. Try telling that to a Victorian mother trying to bring up six children in a tiny space, doing outwork and burdened by truly onerous home chores!

## TOO LAZY TO ENTERTAIN THEIR GUESTS PROPERLY, TOO

Also when the modern British couple entertain they are lazy. Rita Konig explains that 'You don't have to be a good cook to give a dinner party. All you need is a little culinary sleight of hand and a handy selection of good delis.' In her book, aptly titled *Rita's Culinary Trickery* (Ebury, 2004), she advises hosts to buy almost all the food in, just roasting a leg of lamb themselves. She even restricts choice of drinks: 'It's much nicer to be given a drink than to be asked what you want. The fewer decisions the better, to my mind.' On one point, however, Miss Konig is most reactionary. She thinks 'there is no better way of getting people together in a relaxed environment than to invite them to sit around your table'. Do you not know, Miss Konig, that you are expecting Mrs Reader not only to visit the deli and roast a piece of lamb, but, in the case of a quarter of your readers, to splash out and buy a table?

Curiously, time and again, lamb is given as the easy option. Poor dinner party guests must be heartily sick of it. Xanthe Clay in the *Daily Telegraph* (29 October 2005) goes even further than Miss Konig. She suggests not even serving the first course at table at all. Just hand round bread sticks or small cups of soup where people are standing or sitting. 'Follow with a really good piece of roast lamb.' But not for her the leg – that is far too demanding. A rack is better: 'racks are much easier to cook and serve than leg'. We cannot expect a wife and mother to know how to plonk a leg of lamb in the oven or use a carving knife, can we? If even this is too much, why not have a ready meal delivered to your door? Jan Moir in the *Daily Telegraph* (29 August 2005) tried braised veal and rosemary *jus* with *tagliatelle*, pre-cooked and just needing to be reheated. She found the pasta rubbery and the veal tasting like the worst of school dinners. She was 'shocked and appalled by the poor quality and bad value' of this sort of food. I am shocked by the incredible laziness and rudeness of those who order it and inflict it on comparatively innocent guests.

As I said before, much of this is done in the name of liberating the modern lady from the kitchen. But the modern lady cannot be liberated from the kitchen. She does not *need* liberating from the kitchen. For she hardly ever enters the kitchen – at least to cook. She might go in to check the time of Sarah's dancing class on the large notice board, or to water the plants or rearrange the fruit bowl. But, as we have seen, she rarely cooks a proper family meal. And she does not expend much time or effort shopping for food, either. Good French housewives shop for food six times a week: not a complete shop but at least the day's fish and the cheese just right for eating this evening; bread, too, twice a day. The Spanish are more serious and shop twice daily. The English housewife would like to do one big weekly shop at the supermarket. Look at the number of items in the average trolley to see how true this is. In fact, she has to return more frequently. This is not because she wants the mackerel to be fresh, but because she is incompetent and disorganized – as well as lazy. She does not make a thorough list. Research by the retail research company iD Magasin finds 70 per cent shop without lists. And those who have lists only put a few items on them.

The supermarkets are stuffed with ready-to-use vegetables, pre-sliced meats, filleted fish. The modern cook is so lazy she begrudges the few minutes necessary to peel, slice and fillet. Cooking involves a range of basic skills. In addition to slicing, peeling and filleting, there is frying, roasting, baking, liaising, reducing, flouring, amalgamating, drawing, skinning, coating – perhaps a total of fifty skills in all. The cook not only has to be able to do these but to have the educated eye, ear and nose to know when they are being done well. Behind the skills lies organization – the quartermaster's tasks. These all require practice and effort and discipline. Yet even that is not enough, for cooking is a tradition and traditions have to be acquired by watching others and imbibing the values driving them – by a sort of apprenticeship.

The modern Englishwoman would rather think that cooking is a matter of having the right recipe or gadget. For the true requirements of the kitchen are effort and various moral qualities. She does not have these moral qualities and does not care to be reminded of them, still less of her lack of them. Indeed, the fact that she views her kitchen either as a prison or a playground, rather than the moral hub of a happy and well-fed family, is the flaw that exposes all the many others.

## INCOMPETENCE

The moral failing of the English wife and mother as cook means that her cooking will be incompetent. (Lest these charges be construed as idiosyncratic misogyny, I note that Miss Joanna Blythman – an individual with views generally very different to mine – suggests in her recent book *Bad Food Britain* (Fourth Estate, 2006) that the English cook shows 'resistance to devoting any time to food shopping or preparation'.) But in England she is not alone in her incompetence over food. Take her husband, for instance, who makes a ceremonial visit to the kitchen every other month to make his special dish. This is usually something he regards as suitably manly – which means curry. He would rather, of course, not enter the female kitchen at all. The garden is where a chap should be making flames and burning beef on a barbecue. Or take the shopkeepers. Here there really has been a revolution, and all for the worse. Once upon a time the butcher, the fishmonger and even the greengrocer were knowledgeable, skilled people who knew their wares. They went to wholesale markets, looked, probed, inquired and bought. My old butcher used to be able to tell me which carcass a piece of meat came from, how old the animal was, when it had been slaughtered and which field it had lived in. Now a boy in the supermarket looks at the label to find what it is that you are asking for.

The modern English are not just incompetent at cooking food. They don't know how to eat it either. We saw earlier that asparagus is regarded as a treat and thus gets served at dinner parties. Every year I watch people making a hash of eating it. It is not difficult to eat. You pick it up, dunk it in olive oil, mayonnaise, *hollandaise* or whatever, then put the end in your mouth and pull it off with your teeth. The operation is repeated either until the spear is finished or until the teeth encounter fibrous resistance. Not complicated. Yet two guests fool about with knives and forks; two try and consume it all, regardless of the fibres, and wind up having to spit it out discreetly, but not discreetly enough; and the rest take only the first bite and waste the rest of what they themselves regard as a treat. They can't eat fowl with bones. They can't manage pigs' tails. They can't bite the sandbag out of a whelk. They waste most of a prawn: they won't suck the meat and juice from the head, the best taste of all. They massacre the cheese board cutting this way and that. If one is rash enough to serve a first course of a variety of dishes, they take a little of each so they can eat them at the same time. Very often they eat too much of early courses and then can't eat later ones. I have even had guests who come to dinner with no appetite because they have eaten lunch too late.

## OTHER TENDENCIES

Three other tendencies can be despatched much more briefly. The English seem quite unaware that several centuries of able French, Italian, Spanish, Chinese and Indian people have developed quite enough dishes to last anyone a lifetime of eating. The last thing eaters need is new dishes. Every new dish eaten requires the forsaking of an old, great dish. As a result of this quite extraordinary ignorance, they value something that is largely destructive in cooking and eating: novelty. Good cooks make modest demands of their kitchens. All they need is a small room with a cooker, fridge, table, and a couple of small working surfaces, some drawers and a larder. The cooker can be any old four-ring gas model. They want a few good non-stainless steel knives, the odd piece of remainder wood for chopping on, a few iron frying pans – that sort of thing. People who can't cook have 'fitted' kitchens: did I say 'have'? They keep having fitted kitchens, once every five years, with all sorts of expensive and useless equipment. They treat the kitchen as something to show off, not to use. That is because, essentially, they have *contempt for actual cooking.*

The last tendency is a result of all the others. A survey of 2,500 retail outlets, including supermarkets, found that a quarter of assistants do not smile at or make eye contact with shoppers. Supermarkets scored particularly badly on smiling, with 30 per cent of staff not managing it. I'm not surprised. What the survey did not reveal was how miserable shoppers look, shouting at their children, scowling in confusion at the goods, wandering around dazed as if in a dream. Some 70 per cent of them say they hate shopping (for food). Again one is not surprised, given the places they shop at and the food they buy. A real food outing is the greatest pleasure in the world, involving as it does buying foods that will make good dishes and give pleasure, talking with knowledgeable, interesting shopkeepers, discovering things one did not expect to find. In the kitchen, at the shop and even at the table the typical English cook is thoroughly and deservedly *miserable.*

# CHAPTER 4

## SHOPPING: WHAT THE ENGLISH WON'T BUY AND COOK

### WHAT MAKES A GOOD COOK?

The various tendencies discussed in chapter three – meanness, laziness, incompetence, etc. – have the combined effect that the English cannot, or will not, buy and use the ingredients that the great culinary traditions consider essential for good food. I mentioned recently that I was going to dine with some friends, the Richardsons. The person I was talking to asked, 'Will they serve a good dinner? Can they cook?' The answers to the two questions are not necessarily the same. It is just possible that Henry Richardson might send out for food and heat it up, and the results might just be palatable. In France there are some very good *traiteurs* that specialize in ready-prepared dishes. Yet, even if Henry had access to one, we would not say that he had 'cooked' a good dinner. So, clearly just serving good food does not make someone a good cook. Cooking is not just heating dishes up. Obviously the good cook will be good at preparing and combining ingredients. He will also know what to buy and how to keep it in his kitchen before preparation. To answer the second question, 'Is Henry a good cook?' you would not only have to eat Henry's dinner, but see what he does in the kitchen, how he shops, what food he keeps in his fridge, larder and deep freeze, and how he keeps it. If Henry has a garden, one might have a look to see what vegetables and herbs he grows. If he has a field, does he keep a few geese, ducks and hens, and what sort? If he shoots, does he know how to hang, clean and dress game? If he has a salting crock, does he salt his own beef and pork and fish? If he does not have a salting crock, why not? It is all very well saying that preparation and combination of ingredients is a central task of cooking, but even that should be subdivided into preparation for today's dinner and the preparation of basic stocks that will be re-prepared for individual meals. The good cook buys aubergines and peppers when cheap, blanches them and stores them in vinegar and oil for hors d'oeuvres later in the year. He salts anchovies, stores goat's cheese in olive oil, buys in geese when they are available, joints and freezes them, or makes *confit*. He renders pork, duck and beef fat to keep for cooking.

If, then, you want to know whether someone like Henry is a good cook, you need to peer in his fridge, watch him at the butcher's, check his larder, see him at primary and immediate preparation. But what exactly are we looking for?

## SHOPPING

The late Jane Grigson, one of the few thorough English cookery writers, put it like this:

> *I used to think, when I started writing about food…*
> *that salvation lay in improved cookery. Teach everyone*
> *to cook well…and we should be saved. Now I conclude*
> *that salvation lies in shopping, shopping daily for the*
> *best things you can find.*

This is not quite right because, as I have argued, shopping is only part of cooking. But it is surely right in its implication that clever recipes and kitchen techniques are worthless without wisely bought ingredients. There is another implication of worth, too, and it lies in the phrase '[that] you can find'. Shoppers have to accept what they can find, and with food you never know exactly what you *are* going to find. So it cannot be dogmatically pre-planned. Most English cooks shop like Communists. Communists sit in central bureaux and plan what the real and diverse world should look like, then try and force it into their preconceived plan. English cooks, thinking about their coming dinner party, sit at home selecting plans from their cookery books. The ingredients for the recipe are then copied onto a shopping list or committed to memory. The cook sets off to the shops to 'fulfil the plan'. She is instantly stalled by reality. The trout she was going to start with are sold out. The parsley, which was essential, is tired out. The ducks are too big or small for the number of guests. At the same time, the fishmonger has some very good skate and the butcher some rather inexpensive hares; but those were not in the plan. The book that would tell her what to do with them and remind her of the other ingredients necessary to go with them is at home.

A good cook doesn't shop like that. She leaves home with two or three ideas for each course, based on what was available when she was last at the shops. This, of course, as Jane Grigson points out, was yesterday. Good cooks shop daily – not only to ensure freshness but to keep informed of changing items, qualities and prices. The good cook knows what she has in her larder and fridge. She looks at what the butcher or fishmonger has to offer, and with her knowledge of great dishes she constructs a menu:

> *If I buy the skate, it'll need a sauce. That could be*
> beurre noir – *butter, vinegar and a few capers, so I need*
> *a few more capers. However, if we had it like that, we*
> *couldn't use that Spanish recipe for the hare since that*
> *also uses vinegar. Let's jug the hare. In that case I need*
> *a few carrots…*

To shop like this you have to know your shops, recipes, the ingredients required and those already in the larder – and know plenty about each. For instance, not all fish comes from the fishmonger. Salt cod comes from the Italian delicatessen, as will anchovies in oil or salt (unless you have done your own at home). Fish from warmer waters might best be bought from shops owned or patronized by Asians and West Indians. The Chinese shops are good for fish that should be bought live, such as eels and catfish. Obviously fresh fish is usually preferable to frozen, but it is worth finding somewhere for frozen fish as well. Good cooks also go on outings to find ingredients, especially during times of glut. At such times the small fishing ports will often provide herring, mackerel and sprats very cheaply, and the good cook will buy ten pounds or so and salt and preserve them.

It's the same with butchers: good cooks use more than one. The local butcher may provide lamb, beef and pork. Often his bacon will be bought in, mass produced watery nonsense. For bacon you need someone who cures his own. But he won't sell game. That is best bought direct from someone who shoots. The same shoot may not have pheasants and partridges, or the various duck, teal, mallard and widgeon. None of these sources is reliable for chicken, geese and domesticated ducks. For those a farm that keeps them is the best bet. While everyday pork might be bought from an ordinary butcher, specialist pork products come from a pork butcher. For boiling fowl a kosher or halal butcher is the source.

I have said quite enough to demonstrate that establishing sources – and lots of them – is one mark of the good shopper, and that creating menus out of the realities of what is available is another.

## THE NARROW RANGE OF INGREDIENTS THE ENGLISH BUY

However, perhaps the simplest test of a good cook is the range of ingredients she buys and serves. During the year a good cook will buy, prepare and serve most of the following fish:

anchovies
angler (monk)
*baccala* (salt cod)
bass (not farmed)
breams (various)
calamari (squid)
carp
clams (various)
cockles
cod
conger eel
crab
cuttlefish
dogfish
eels
elvers
fish heads and bones
(for fish soup)
flounder
garfish
grey mullet
gurnard
haddock
hake
halibut
herring
John Dory
kippers
lamprey
limpet
lobster
mackerel

mussels
octopus
oyster
perch
pike
plaice
prawns
red mullet
salmon
salt fish (other than cod)
sardines
scallops
sea urchins
shark
shrimps
skate
smoked fish
(e.g. mackerel, cod roe)
snapper (various)
sole (various)
sprat
swordfish
tench
trout (brown only)
tuna
turbot
weever
whelk
whitebait
whiting
winkle

It may be that a particular cook disapproves of one or two of these and cannot get another three or four of them, but fifty to sixty of them should be on her list and table. If there are fewer than 20 over the year, she is no cook at all. Several of them are inexpensive. Winkles are free to anyone living near a rocky coast. Yet I see no one else gathering them as I do. Fish heads from the frequently filleted fish such as cod and haddock are more or less free. They form the basis of fish soups and the stocks without which many of the best fish dishes are impossible. Yet they are daily thrown away by fishmongers. Gurnard provides solid flesh for a variety of sauced fish dishes, yet it is spurned. Crabs, still quite cheap, are rarely served, and the few people who do serve them buy them in the wrong way. Instead of buying crabs live, and boiling and cleaning and preparing them themselves, they buy pre-dressed crabs, which dry and stale rapidly. Salt cod, which the sensible cooks of all the Mediterranean countries value enormously, is rarely bought in England. Here, for instance, are a few of the salt cod dishes that the English cook regularly deprives her guests of:

*brandade*
(creamed with milk and olive oil and garlic)
*bunyols*
(Catalan fritters of a *brandade*-type mixture)
slivers, raw with oil and garlic
with tomato and herbs
with potatoes, saffron and black olives
floured and fried
baked with potatoes and milk
stewed with onions
stewed in olive oil and garlic, then as a sauce on pasta
stuffed in peppers

And here is what the guests are not allowed to eat when the very cheap garfish is in season:

short segments floured and fried
poached, filleted and jellied in its own broth
with added gelatine to make false jellied eels
fillets cooked in butter and chicken stock with parsley
poached with onions, leeks and chives
fried in olive oil with garlic
with sorrel

The English appear to reject the garfish entirely. With food such as mussels, it is a different story. They embrace them and serve them always in the same tedious way, *à la marinière*. Here are other, better ways they refuse to countenance:

best of all, raw
with garlic and chillies on pasta
stuffed with minced pork
in mussel risotto
grilled with clams
with egg yolk sauce
in *gratin* with spinach
in black bean sauce

Nor is it a defence to argue that fish is difficult to buy because fishmongers are few and far between. On the contrary, fishmongers are few in number because the English buy little fish – far less than the Mediterraneans – and limit themselves to a very restricted range. We live in a society in which families will drive an hour to visit shopping temples for the most fashionable jeans or gadgets, but will make no effort to find and buy fish.

## AND THE RANGE OF MEAT THE GOOD COOK COULD BUY

Ours is a culture that flatly rejects the best in meat, as well as fish. Meat available in England falls under ten broad categories:

| | |
|---|---|
| beef | ground game (hares |
| veal | and wild rabbits) |
| lamb | game birds |
| mutton | (pheasants, partridge, |
| goat | grouse and, for |
| pork | convenience, pigeons, |
| poultry | wild mallard, teal, |
| (chickens, | widgeon, snipe, woodcock) |
| domesticated ducks | *charcuterie* (for cooking, |
| and geese and quail; | chiefly bacon and hams, |
| also we might | but also salt pork, |
| conveniently add here | sausages, black and |
| domesticated rabbit) | white puddings) |

The first few on the list generate sub-categories by method of cooking or further preparation. Thus there is roasting pork, stewing pork, frying pork, mincing pork for fresh sausages, stuffing, etc. For some of them we should add further sub-categories of offal and extremities (liver, kidneys, tongues, tails, etc.). And for each of these categories there are at least five great recipes. To cut a long story short, if you were to list the top five recipes for all the various different sorts of meats and game on the list you would have well over a hundred dishes. As with the fish, we would expect the competent cook to produce a wide range of these dishes, and to source and buy a wide range of the different cuts and types of meat. Add the fish and meat together and there is no reason why any such cook need serve the same dish more than two or three times a year for dinner. She might wish to, of course. And some of her

guests might wish her to: I certainly demand kidneys and pigs'
tails at least once a month. But you get the point: there are lots
of great and well-known dishes available to the shopper and
cook. And yet, as with fish, we see the same old favourites
being served up: steak, roast leg or shoulder of lamb, pork
chops. That is boring and bad enough, but again, as with fish,
what is rejected is even more serious. Some of the very best
beef dishes are made with stewing or braising beef:

*bordelaise*, with shallots, red wine, tarragon,
mushrooms, marrowbone

*bourguignon*, with salt pork, onions, stock

*pebronata*, with oil, wine and juniper berries

*stiphado*, with wine and tomato

*daube*
1. with wine, carrots, bacon, black olives, garlic
2. minus olives, but with thyme and lemon peel
and served with turnips
3. with anchovies
4. with pigs' trotters
5. as for 4 but with more trotters
and served cold and jellied
6. with ceps, fresh or dried
7. *gascon*, with armagnac

Replace the wine with beer and you have *carbonade*.

Replace the wine with tomato or puréed dried peppers
and that's the base for a whole lot more dishes.

All these can be varied by changing the fat involved,
olive oil, goose fat, *chorizo* fat, etc.

Every nationality also seems to have a dish of
boiled beef, from *pot-au-feu* to *bollito* to boiled beef
and carrots with dumplings.

Stewing and braising beef is also the beef that is
minced for all dishes needing ground beef.
It is the beef that goes into pies and puddings as well.

### OPPORTUNITY COSTS IN THE KITCHEN

Economists have a concept termed 'opportunity cost'. Every time you do something, the opportunity cost is all the other things you could have done. Every time the English cook serves up another dreary steak or chop, she is depriving her family and friends of dishes like those above. It is as if she were shown an Aladdin's cave, a treasury of all that is best in the gastronomic world, only for her to reply, 'I think I'll stick with chops.' Besides depriving diners of great dinners, her incredible ingratitude has a further consequence. Because she won't buy three-quarters of what is available, the price of these cuts and types of meat tumbles. Every couple of weeks I ask my butcher for pigs' tails. They are poached, then grilled till crispy and are eaten with garlic and parsley. He gives them to me because no one else wants them except the odd Chinese. The same with beef suet for dumplings. Beef kidneys cost a fifth of what steak costs. Ox liver costs less per serving than one small cigarette. Week after week the tedious poverty lobby rants about the need to give more handouts to the poor. But the English are so determined to reject the good things provided for the table by the Almighty that, even when poor, they won't eat dishes that the French or Spanish would pay good Euros for.

So the sight of Henry Richardson and his compatriots at the butcher and the fishmonger provides the strongest evidence for the case that the English still cannot and will not cook properly. Let's go indoors for the next spot of evidence. What is in Henry's larder?

### IN THE LARDER, THE FRIDGE AND THE FREEZER

The answer, of course, is lots of tins and even more packets. We were kind to the English cook out shopping when we suggested that she bought only a few of the types of meat available and rejected the rest. In fact, generally speaking, most of the time she spurns all fresh, unprepared meat or fish. She prefers to buy packets of processed foods, which she heats up in a microwave. So lazy is she that she cannot even make a sandwich or pizza herself. What should be in the larder of the good cook? At least most of the following:

tea
coffee
sugar, various
split peas
chickpeas
lentils (green, pink and white)
rice (Arborio, Valencia, basmati, Thai and glutinous)
strong flour (for bread), plain flour, chickpea flour
pasta (for both boiled and oven dishes)
dried peppers, dried tomatoes
French *saucisson*
Italian salami
Italian or Spanish ham
dried anchovies
salad and cooking olive oil (gallons)
black and green olives in brine
tins of tomatoes
wine vinegar
Tabasco

Most of these are bought as they are. But the larder will also contain various preserves the cook has made. They would include:

cod, salted at home
herrings, salted at home
peppers, blanched in wine vinegar then stored in oil
aubergines the same way
a mixed pickle of onion, celery, cucumbers, turnip and carrots

> pickled onions
> red cabbage
> homemade *kimchee*
> anchovies, bought on holiday abroad, salted in
> the hotel bathroom then brought back and
> stored in olive oil with dried chilli flakes

Thinking about these two lists, you can see how they point to the sort of cooking the cook has already done and will do. A larder with few of these things is no larder and indicates that the owner is no cook. In fact, this does not apply in Henry's case because he, like an increasing number of the English, has no larder at all. What few of these items he has, he crams into his enormous fridge. The space his larder would have taken up is absorbed by yet another bathroom. You can tell the priorities of the modern English by the allocation of rooms in their houses. Top is showering and protecting their cars. Bottom is cooking – or at least true cooking.

Most of the things in Henry's fridge do not need to be there. Some will not be at their best on account of being there. Apart from butter, milk, champagne and other things used every day, the fridge should really be kept to store meat and fish from the time it is bought till the time it is cooked – a matter of hours since cooks shop every day – and to store the cooked meat and fish from after dinner till next day, when something will be done to it. It is a brief resting place, not a permanent home. Depending on the temperature outside, the fridge or larder will also be the place to store the various rendered cooking fats (beef for chips, goose, duck and pork) and briefly for stocks (chicken, pork, veal and fish) before they are used or stored in the deep freeze.

It is obvious to anyone who has read one of the standard French cookery books that cooking without the right fats and stocks is simply impossible. When you go and stay with relatives or friends don't bother to inspect the many bathrooms. Just look in the fridge or larder for the basic stocks and fats. If they are not there, leave, shake the dust from your feet, and curse the place and those who dwell therein!

Had this book been written twenty years ago the deep freeze might have escaped without a mention. Nowadays it is indispensable. Because of the decline in the number of butchers and fishmongers, the good cook must buy good things when and where she can find them. Having found them she will buy in some quantity. Obviously she will only buy in quantity those things that freeze or can be preserved well in some other way. The freezer will be full of white fish and crabs but not much oily fish. It will have pheasants and partridges (after they have been hung) but not hares. It will have ducks and geese but not lamb; tripe and tails but not kidneys and testicles. And the good cook will monitor its contents. That white fish especially wants to be in there only a matter of weeks.

## CROCKS, *POTAGERS* AND PADDOCKS

Most good cooks will run a crock for at least the winter months to wet salt pork and beef. Not all good cooks will own or have access to a vegetable garden, but many will. It should have in it those things that are sometimes difficult to get in shops. Not potatoes or onions, but rocket, *frisée*, spinach, small turnips, sorrel, celeriac. If one is lucky enough to have a small field or paddock then obviously it will be full of geese, ducks and chickens. A goat is a possibility and so is a pig. Put it this way, if one saw a house with a field and it was given over to flower bulbs or vintage cars, one would know one was not at the home of a cook.

## CHAPTER 5

## THE REJECTION OF GOOD FOOD

### THE AMOUNT OF WASTE

According to the Waste and Resources Action Programme, the average person throws away £424 worth of food a year. There is an interesting side-effect of this colossal waste. Most of the statistics about what England eats – and these are the figures that supposedly justify all the government regulations and nannying and health scares – are based on what people buy. If they waste much of this, and, crucially, we don't know which items they leave, then the statistics are useless and so are the regulations.

With younger people, the waste comes about not only because they don't know their own appetites or are fastidious. It is because they get bored. For any activity in their wretched instant sensation-seeking lives, their attention span is so short that the chips they desired so greatly three minutes ago now bore them. I once patrolled a cross-Channel ferry to see what 'they' eat and how. 'They' had plenty of time to eat: the ferries are more or less as slow now as they were half a century ago. What the young people queuing up for their food wanted were sausages, beans and chips. The first thing they did when they sat down with their plates, on which were piled reasonably crispy chips, two sausages and a separate mound of beans, was to squeeze on tomato sauce. They then proceeded to swirl the sauce, beans and chips into a mush. Just like mud pies. Within ten minutes they had finished. The average amount left was a third.

## MRS DAVID'S DEFORMITY OF A COW

The rejection of food was mentioned briefly in chapter three under the heading of squeamishness. It now time we gave it more sustained attention. Why? Because there is another, crucial, aspect to it. It is not only that food is rejected, with the waste of money that entails; but it is good food that is rejected. That is the puzzle: why so many English people, children, young people and adults reject what other and nobler food cultures have found to be good. The late, famous British food writer Elizabeth David once invited her readers to picture a cow. Not just any sort of cow: this was a special cow – or bull – a misshapen abomination of the species *bos*. It is standing, but not on its hooves, for it is lacking hooves. Its feet have been cut off just below the knee. It has no belly, no stomach, no horns, indeed no head at all; and no heart, no lungs, liver, pancreas or kidneys. One might suppose this to be a gory sight but in fact it is not, for the cow has no blood. It has also been skinned and it has no fat either. To compensate for its lack of head, stomach and blood, this cow has an extra amount of certain other parts. Most noticeably, and overshadowing all else, is the most enormous bottom wobbling on two huge hind thighs. Though it might be called an 'Elizabeth David cow', it would better be called a 'consumer cow' because it is what a cow would look like if it consisted only of the parts that the English consumer would wittingly buy.

The English consumer doesn't want the heart to stew in red wine or the liver to soak in milk then braise with onions. She doesn't want the suet fat to make dumplings to go with the stewing cuts (which she doesn't want either). Even in the days when the government allowed her to buy the brains and sweetbreads and cheek, she would not have those either. So when it started to interfere and ban things, she did not raise a voice in protest. And, of course, she cannot be bothered to wash and clean tripes or long-cook those feet. What she does want is beef for steaks and beef for roasting. She does, in fact, buy many other bits, but only unwittingly, since they are minced to the point of being unrecognizable or are concealed in pies and processed dishes.

What the David cow illustrates, among other things, is just how many good things the English consumer rejects. By 'good' I mean ingredients that are valued by better food cultures – and indeed, in some cases, were once valued here. One could also imagine a 'consumer fish' – no head, no bones, no tail, no roes, no skin – swimming in a consumer sea teeming with large striped prawns – also headless, of course. Cod and tuna steaks would slip serenely through the water, unimpeded by any common cuttlefish, whelks or dogfish. The prospect of dogfish done Spanish-style in *adobo*, with vinegar and fried; of cuttlefish with garlic and ink, or of whelks in a chilli sauce does not entice her at all. What! She, spend her time poaching, filleting, cleaning fish or taking the sandbags out of whelks? Pull the other one!

## WASTE IN THE KITCHEN

The quantity and sheer variety of food spurned and wasted in England is enormous. It takes place obviously in the shops and, since the shopkeeper knows what his customers won't buy, he refuses the produce from his suppliers. Three things happen to the rejected ingredients. When possible they are sold in the UK or abroad at fair prices to people who have the taste and competence and commitment to appreciate and prepare them. Some are hidden in processed foods. Yet others are again sold, but at prices that reflect the lack of demand. This is the only good consequence of this sorry tale: that many of the foods spurned are now extremely cheap, particularly certain fish, game and offal. Thus the shopkeepers reject good things at source, and the housewives reject good things in the shops.

But they also reject things at home. It is difficult to gauge the amount of waste that goes on in the average kitchen. Some guesstimates suggest a third. It is probably higher, because now that families do not eat together often, and the choice of food and its preparation on any day is not under the control of any one family member, any form of planned consumption is bound to go haywire. Then there is waste on 'the plate'. There are three forms of this. Teenage Jake takes a packet of something from the fridge or deep freeze and microwaves it. He puts it on a surface – the table, his school books, the video, his discarded trainers, the car roof; in fact, anything but a plate – and starts to eat. Halfway through he gets 'bored' – either with it or just with the prolonged effort with chewing. Perhaps some other activity takes his fancy. The remainder is left to congeal on his trainers. Again, at a rare family meal at table – as documented earlier, many English families no longer have dining tables or else use them for something other than eating – Mum might dish out portions onto plates in fixed amounts, and someone will find they don't want this or don't fancy that and will push it to the side of the plate. Most curious of all, at the rare formal meal where food is served in central dishes and individual diners help themselves or are helped by the host to amounts according to their expressed wishes, diners still leave food. It must be either that they have forgotten what lamb, peas, bacon or whatever tastes like when they accept it, or that they have lost the basic ability to estimate how hungry they are. Maybe they just can't be bothered with the once-simple business of eating.

Why do the English reject all this food? It is not hard to see why food in the kitchen gets wasted or is pushed to the side of the plate. The sloppy, self-indulgent, bad-mannered and ungrateful attitude of so many people, especially the young, to food has already been mentioned. But why are whole classes of food – offal and extremities, 90 per cent of the fish in the sea – and a large proportion of the techniques and recipes for preparing them rejected? They are rejected by those who might have been expected to buy and cook them and by those who might have been expected to eat and enjoy them. The eaters reveal their main reasons for rejecting good food when they shudder, 'Oh, I couldn't!' or register their amazement, 'Eat brains? Don't be ridiculous!' One reason we have mentioned is squeamishness. Another is an intense conservatism. The conservatism is bizarre. They will try out cocaine but not sweetbreads. The squeamishness is childish and sentimental: a distaste of the viscous (the slimy whelk and frothing sticky *escargot*), of the bloody *civet*, of strong smells, the grassy tripe, the ripe hung woodcock. There is a special distaste of anything dead that resembles something that might have been cute when alive.

## THE PECULIARITY OF THE ENGLISH DISTASTE FOR GOOD FOOD

Once again, we have to emphasize how very peculiar this distaste is. The French simply do not reject food in this way. Of course, individual French people, Italians and Spaniards have their preferences; but their populations do not reject whole classes of food in this way. All food that is hallowed by tradition is good. The main explanation of why the English reject good food is that they have neither the competence nor the commitment and energy to prepare it. Before looking at the nature of this moral lethargy, let's look more closely at the incompetence.

## A DEFICIENT REPERTOIRE

The French have a cookery book known as an *abrégé de cuisine*. The dictionary translates *abrégé* as 'abridgement' and that makes sense because an *abrégé* lists in summary the ways of cooking various ingredients. Look up pigs' feet and it will briefly tell you that it can be done *bourgeoise*, poached and finished with Madeira; *gratin*, breadcrumbed, with white wine, herbs, shallots, butter and *gratiné*; *huile*, poached, sauce *vinaigrette*, etc. Look up mackerel and you find *anglaise*, grilled or poached, served with potatoes and melted butter;

*fines herbes*, poached, white wine sauce and herbs; *meunière*, fried, herbs, butter, lemon, etc. If one were to create a Mediterranean *abrégé* with Spanish and Italian treatments as well as the French, the treatments per ingredient might average some 12 to 50. And there are hundreds of ingredients. It is this knowledge that the competent cook needs; an appreciation of the suitable treatment for ingredients and the technical skill and practice to do it. It is not quite as daunting as it first sounds, because there is a good deal of duplication and the differences between two treatments can be minor – but crucial – as the mackerel example shows.

## AN *ABRÉGÉ* FOR THE MARKET

This knowledge, however, is not the only knowledge the cook needs. Think what an *abrégé du marché* might look like – a shopping abridgement. For each ingredient it would explain, in summary, how to discern and buy the best quality, how to tell the difference between apparently similar types, and what else to buy to accompany whatever it is. Thus, under 'Tomatoes', it might say 'origin is more important than type, they must come from sunny countries where they ripen quickly and countries with earth, above all not from Holland; it is the flesh that is important, as one is not buying pith, pips and a pretty skin; to cook stuffed, buy also pork, herbs, garlic...'

I prefer to use the term 'repertoire' to describe the stock of regularly used knowledge both of shopping and cooking. It is this repertoire that the competent cook possesses and the incompetent one lacks. To tease its character out a little further, take one category: birds. The competent cook will know how to buy and cook young chickens, old 'boiling' birds, chicken livers, necks and feet, domestic duck, teal, widgeon and mallard, duck's liver, stuffed necks, feet, wild pigeons, squabs, quail, turkeys, geese, partridge, pheasants, black game, woodcock, snipe and rooks. For each there are immediate treatments that average perhaps half a dozen per bird.

'Immediate' because there are long-term treatments, first cooking and cooking for preservation; almost all the birds can be made into *pâté* and terrine. Some are fit for sausages fresh or cured, some for smoking. Every competent cook needs to have an awareness of, and a gratitude for, the sheer abundance and huge variety of foods the Almighty has given us to eat, and an awareness of the skills and traditions that the pinnacle of his creation, Man, has evolved to prepare them.

And yet, at the butcher's, I hear a lady bleat, 'Oh dear, what shall I have? We had beef yesterday and chops on Saturday; what can I have?' as if she had exhausted the ingredients available. There are clearly households in England where the cook's repertoire is a fiftieth of what it should be; households where only two cuts of beef are used and are cooked in only one way apiece; households where game and wild meats, offal and extremities, and shellfish never darken the threshold. Not only are these people incompetent and failing their families in a disgraceful way, but they are ungrateful. Instead of praising the Almighty for his abundance and instead of reverencing the great traditions of cooking, they treat food as a chore, an imposition: 'What shall we have?'

### DISCIPLINE, EFFORT AND PRACTICE

There are, to be sure, some dishes that are used every day or very frequently. Bread in French cooking is eaten every day, and much the same bread, too. Many 'Asians' eat rice every day. This, and the fact that many of the treatments of ingredients are common or vary only slightly, means that the cook who cooks every day, 365 days a year, also gets lots of practice. I suppose many middle-aged Asian ladies have cooked rice 50,000 times. My wife has made bread over 1,000 times. The modern English cook often complains how difficult she finds some of these tasks: 'My rice never comes out right' or 'My bread is always hard.' To solve her problems she constantly buys new cookery books or searches for new recipes and willingly laps up the many dollops of advice on techniques that are 'magic' and sure to succeed. Indeed, her attitude to cookery books and recipes smacks of the worst sort of magic: 'If I buy the book and take it home and read it, surely that will in itself make my rice fluffy and separate.'

What she does not do, will not do, is the one thing that would help – practise. Practice comes in two ways. The way to perfect a new dish is to practise, as though in a laboratory. You want to learn to make Spanish omelette? Find any old standard recipe, buy the right ingredients and enter the kitchen. One crucial ingredient will be a cat or dog. Make the omelette ten times, varying the timing and the quantities. Throw the worst failures away and give the rest to the cat or dog. You may now be ready to inflict a not-too-bad omelette on your family. A year and several family omelettes later, you might risk it on your friends.

The second sort of practice comes from shopping and cooking regularly at home. The good cook shops every day and cooks at least twice a day. It is just not possible to snack and microwave your way through the week and cook only once, on Sunday. A good kitchen depends on an accumulation of ingredients regularly replenished, fresh herbs, stocks, last night's *daube* served tomorrow for a first course *en gelée*. With cooking the rule is simple: do it often or never.

## THE MODERN LADY IS TOO BUSY TO BOTHER WITH MERE FOOD

The modern rejoinder to such arguments is that the lady of today has no time to shop and cook. I have watched the modern lady shopping. I have seen her sitting in traffic jams on her way to the out-of-town supermarket, her preference for which has destroyed local shops and small traders. I have watched her gossiping with friends outside the supermarket. I have observed her wandering around these supermarkets, piling her trolley. She buys a lot, but not systematically. A recent survey showed that only a minority of people use a list. She takes things from shelves in a haphazard way, and this is occasionally made worse by impulse and sentimental, ill-disciplined concessions to the imprecations of whining children. What I *don't* see in her behaviour is the organized, efficient raid of someone desperately short of time. It is not that she won't shop. On the contrary, she loves shopping, and spends lots of time and money on it. She is forever shopping for clothes, fashions, children's goods. She is forever at the hairdresser or in the mall. It is *food* shopping that she refuses to make the subject of disciplined effort.

Surveys also show that she cannot manage her finances prudently: she has higher debts than ever before, though she has more to spend than any previous generation. She spends a lot of time watching television, staring at her mobile 'phone and under the shower. She has the time to shop, if she were committed to food shopping. But she isn't. As for time to cook, it needs to be emphasized that good, competent cooking does not take a lot of time, but it does require the ordered use of time. Making bread requires one to make the dough some time before baking it, but the actual making of the dough takes three minutes. The baking may take longer, but *you* don't have to do that: the oven can be left to do it on its own. Similarly, slicing up some stewing beef and onions for a stew takes a couple of minutes, and then the oven does the rest.

Contemporary food journalists and women's magazines flatter their readers by telling them how good they are; reassuring them that it's fine to use shortcuts and even deceit in cooking; confiding to them that they *know* just how busy they are. It is all – to invoke something no modern lady would bother with – tripe.

It is a sociological truism that, as an organization loses its true and original purpose, its hierarchy becomes bigger, its offices grander and its status symbols more ostentatious. Just as today's home cook more or less gives up cooking proper meals, except once or twice a week, so her kitchen gets grander, her cooker gets larger, her equipment flashier and more advanced. There it is – the £5,000 refitted kitchen, the £1,000 cooker, the fridge that the family can fit in, the machine for this and that, its proprietress in a chef's hat, and the poor dear turns out one twentieth of the meals her grandmother cooked! Decline and fall are not confined to empires, and nor are bread and circuses.

## AND WHAT OF MEN?

Talking of circuses brings us to *men*. Pretentiousness, inefficiency and tenth-rate food are, usually, the fault of women. That is, it is women who largely do the shopping and cooking and are therefore to blame for the appalling standards that prevail in most homes. Men, in a sense, are worse. They simply do next to nothing in the kitchen or in the way of food shopping. If this book spends more time criticizing women than men, it is because you cannot make any detailed criticism of people who do nothing. That does not mean they are not to blame; simply there is less to say about them. Most obviously they are to blame for not helping their wives and mistresses more. And when they do help they make just as poor a fist of it. Studies of food shopping find that men are even more extravagant than their wives or mistresses. In the kitchen they are even more self-indulgent, selecting just one or two jobs best suited for a performance. These usually involve flames and bangs. It's a show. 'Richard always does the curry; he loves doing his curry' or 'Dad's going to do his chilli on Saturday.' There's a lot of display and prima-donna behaviour: 'Please, I can't have you fiddling with the salad in the kitchen while I'm doing my chilli' or 'I can't cook my curry properly in a frying pan, so I've ordered a *tava* and a *karhai* from those speciality mail-order people.'

## AND THE POOR?

Much of the above might be thought to be applicable to the middle class – all this showing off about food while not actually making an organized effort to deliver it on a daily basis. And its culmination is surely in the 'dinner party'. Do precious little serious shopping or cooking for a fortnight, then spend a fortune and hope that extravagance, the predictable wares of the delicatessen and alcohol will conceal the lack of knowledge, effort, practice and commitment. What, though, of those with less money, the unemployed, students, the poorer pensioners? Where's the morality in their kitchens?

In fact, we know rather more about how they spend their money on food and what they cook than we do about the middle classes. This is because, as 'disadvantaged' people, they attract the research, and the political interest, of socialist social-policy academics, charities and welfare lobbyists. These, being socialists, always reach the same conclusion, which is that the poor, pensioners, students, unemployed are forced through penury to eat boring diets lacking in nutrition. Fortunately, in describing the parlous state of the oppressed masses, the researchers are forced to describe what these masses actually do. They buy a lot of processed foods, even though these are, on average, three times the price of foods cooked from raw. They go to the nearest shops regardless of price. They do not budget. Some – students – eat out at three times the cost of eating in. Worst of all, they do not use the one great advantage most of them have: the *time* to shop and cook. They have even more time than the 'busy' middle classes. Especially the unemployed. But they do not use it to cook. Indeed, one study finds them watching television and staying in bed.

It has long been known that some poor people climb out of poverty and others sink deeper into it. The difference between them is that those who get out have a deeper commitment to self-improvement, a horror of debt and better management. These are particularly important with food, since, in low-income families, it accounts for a much greater proportion of the overall expenditure – upwards of 30 per cent. If middle-class families don't bother to shop and cook properly, waste money on extravagant foods, show off with their redundant kitchens, and put their Edwardian-reproduction picnic hampers to use once a year, it does not much affect anyone but those invited to the picnic. (Though it is also a bit hard on the children being brought up without taste and competence in food.) But it is a much more serious thing for the poor. And, for those who follow a consequentialist ethics, this makes the bad behaviour of the poor with their food all the more immoral.

## THE RISE OF NEW ANTI-FOOD VALUES

It should not be assumed that, just because the modern home cook is lazy, ill-disciplined, wasteful and uncommitted, she (or he) has no values at all. A forthcoming Social Affairs Unit study suggests that modern society, while discarding well-tried moral standards, has also acquired new ones. Society is 'decadent' not because it has no standards but because it has exchanged good old ones for worthless new ones. This bad exchange can be seen in the kitchen and market, too. The contemporary consumer has a particularly keen appetite for one thing and that is safety. She is in a permanent panic that this or that food might do her and her family some harm: a UK pressure group neatly encapsulated this in its name, Parents for Safe Food. The mania for safety does not lead her into more hygienic habits in her fridge, of course; safety is the government's business and she constitutes an ever ready con-stituency for regulation. It is the power of this constituency that has allowed the UK government to force small-scale egg producers, cheese producers, shellfish sellers and slaughter-houses out of business, thus drastically reducing the variety and worth of available ingredients. 'Health' is another new value. The modern woman falls for any diet proclaimed to be healthy. The most long lived of these is the Mediterranean diet, which bears no resemblance to anything the Spanish and French actually eat: have the proponents of this diet used their eyes and seen the contents of a French *charcuterie* and cheese shop, or watched the Spanish at breakfast, smearing pork fat on their toast with a Marlboro and sipping a *con leche* saturated with sugar, or possibly a brandy or anise? She is keen on the new business value of 'transparency' and third-party assurance. Being too ignorant and lazy to know how to identify good ingredients, she wants some bureaucracy to do this for her. The power of these third-party bureaucracies also lowers variety and quality. Above all, she believes in the value of self-affirmation and feeling good about herself. Among the acres of newsprint on food, no columnist dare tell her the simple truth – that it is she who is failing in the kitchen. She is, after all, the reader, and the reader must be pandered to. She is also a woman, and the politically correct newspaper knows it cannot make uncomplimentary remarks about women. Curiously, even those feminists who deny any interest in cooking and who refer to their sisters being 'chained to the cooker' resent it if their competence is belittled. It is as if women claim a natural competence in the kitchen. In chapter 9 we consider at length the anti-food ideologies.

## VICE IN THE KITCHEN

The modern age would like to believe that producing a good meal is a knack, a trick that can be turned when one has the time or inclination for it; when it is 'our turn to have the Richardsons and Greys'. To turn the trick, one might find a glossy cookbook useful, and surely if one spends enough on mail-order smoked reindeer that must work. But it is just not like that. It requires a moral vocabulary to understand the making of a good meal. The key words are *respect* for tradition; *knowledge*, or rather *wisdom*; *competence*; *practice*;

*gratitude*; and *commitment*. Decent cultures know there are few higher callings than that of providing good food for one's family and one's guests. This society, for all its noisy celebration of chefs and restaurants, does not know this. Modern culture also has a rather boy's-own attitude to morality. It likes to think that only startling acts can be immoral. In fact, most serious sins are humdrum. No doubt it will be astonished to be told in this book that the behaviour of many modern cooks in their own homes is *vicious*.

## CHAPTER 6

# RESTAURANTS AND RESTAURANT REVIEWS

### A FRENCH VIEW OF ENGLISH FOOD

In the summer of 2005 there was a minor diplomatic incident when the French president was uncomplimentary about British food. The British press reacted with incredulity: did the president not know that British food was among the best in the world now? He had simply shown himself to be out of date; it might once have been poor, but now was a world leader. The English food writers jostled with each other to be the first to say – and to say loudest of all – that British food was wonderful. They went further. It was better than French food because it was more inventive. The French had committed the most awful sin in the eyes of contemporary culture. They had failed to 'move on'. Their food was dull. By way of evidence, the English food writers presented the names of several chefs who were world class and British.

### THE STATE OF ENGLISH FOOD HAS NOTHING TO DO WITH THE STATE OF A FEW EXPENSIVE RESTAURANTS

Forget the French president – which is not difficult (this particular one has no notable achievements to his name). Forget the actual incident. What is interesting is the confounding by British writers of British food with the products of a few London restaurants. British food is what is eaten at home; those hamburgers eaten on the street; the food thrown away in British hospitals and scorned in half the nation's schools. It is also restaurant food, but that eaten in thousands of Tandoori and Chinese restaurants, kebab houses and hamburger places, in second-rate hotels, in marquees at weddings and in cold church halls at funerals.

What a few very expensive London restaurants and their celebrity chefs serve to food journalists, TV and cinema trash and expense-account business people has next to nothing to do with the state of 'British food'. However, what those restaurant reviewers *write* about the celebrity restaurants is interesting. It may only be about a minority of unrepresentative restaurants, but it is written for millions of readers and it says something about the food values of both writers and readers.

## HOW THE ENGLISH WRITE ABOUT RESTAURANT FOOD

The first thing one notices is the language. This is most obvious in hyperbole. Dishes are described in 'quality newspapers' such as *The Times* and the *Telegraph* as 'piss-poor' and 'terrible', or 'stunning', 'sublime', 'stonking' or 'sensationally creative and vibrant'. But it is not just hyperbole. The writing is over-blown, yet the information conveyed is meagre. The best reviewers of books or plays do not write as these people do. But there is one person worse than these extravagant writers; one person even less informative: the chum they take. Generous editors allow restaurant reviewers to take to the restaurants they review someone traditionally identified as 'my companion'. In these days of openness, the companion may be revealed as a spouse or partner and may even be given a name. Whether he likes it or not, the reader is going to be given the opinion of these people as well.

So one prominent reviewer tells us that 'my brother-in law raved about his salmon and basil tikka' (*Sunday Telegraph*, 18 January 2004). Who takes responsibility for this: the brother-in-law for 'raving' or the writer for so uninformative a description? Someone else in the same party gave a careful and educated opinion about the chicken korma: 'It's delicious, it's soooo delicious.' And here, reported in *The Sunday Times*

HEATH

(17 January 2004), is what another party of four made of pumpkin *velouté* (good cooks know that pumpkins have only one use, and that is for American children to play with in the dark in October or November):

> '*Mmmm mmmm, lovely*' *(Andrew).* '*Sweet.
> Delicious*' *(Janette).* '*Velvety*' *(husband, Bruce).*

The columnist, and leader of this group, brings up the rear, but is not to be outdone in precise description:

> '*Gorgeous*' *(Me).*

While we are on language, here are a few more gems from these quality columns:

> *...the food was small but perfectly formed...
> larger quantities would have been* de trop.

> *The roast Shropshire partridge [are Shropshire ones
> any different from those in the rest of the country?]
> managed to be both deliciously dirty and hallucinogenic
> with dusky dribbles of caper and raisin sauce...
> a crescent moon of pumpkin.*

Pumpkin again! Partridge seems to bring out the worst in the writers: another praising the daily freshness of the dishes cites partridge as the lead example. But a good partridge would have been hung (in January, when this was published, for 10 days or so) and has no need to be fresh, let alone fresh daily. The same writer, trying to describe the secret of the 'special brilliance' of his lamb cutlets, explains that the 'taste of lamb and the taste of clay from the tandoor coexisted perfectly'. Set aside, if you can, the 'coexisted perfectly' – does he think he is describing a bilateral agreement between previously warring nations? – I know tandoors are made of clay, but what is this taste of clay?

This particular chap can be relied on for a gem. In another column he writes of 'a huge plate of plump prawns almost beyond counting'. Prawns are not like restaurant critics. They are not, usually, plump or lean, just big or small. (But then plump and prawn both begin with 'p'.) And 'almost beyond counting'? One knows modern schooling standards are poor, but surely he could manage to get up to a dozen or so! And on it goes. These countless prawns are – guess what? – 'drizzled in a creamy, zingy, champagne dressing'. Unfortunately, his crab 'lacked the luxuriance, but was splendidly fresh, the sweetness…cutely relieved by slices of sharp green apple and a cumin crisp'. 'Cutely'? Enough already!

## THE LACK OF AGREED STANDARDS AND LANGUAGE FOR DESCRIBING FOOD

In French there is an adjective *correct* and a phrase, *comme il faut*. *Correct* has roughly the same meanings as the English word, 'correct'. It can mean 'true' or 'right', as in 'four is the correct answer to two plus two'. It can also refer to manners, as in 'correctly dressed'. In both languages the word means 'right' or 'appropriate' as agreed by educated opinion. In France, I have regularly heard restaurants and their dishes described as *correct*. I have never heard it so used in England. To describe a restaurant as *correct* in France is to say one of two things: either that it is appropriate for its class, its situation and its price; or that it is *only* appropriate, and no more than one should expect. Said of a dish, *comme il faut* indicates that it is made as it should be; as everyone who knows expects the dish to be made; even, as it always has been made. Only in a culture that has sophisticated shared ideas about what a dish should be could expressions such as these be used in this way about food. At least until recently, this shared culture existed in France. Everyone – who matters – knew what a *choucroute*, a *Niçoise*, a *soubise*, a *daube*, a *navarin*, a *bourride*, a *pâté de tête*, a *boudin* (black or white) should be. In rather a similar way, Italians know what shape and type of pasta goes with what sauce. It is this notion of, and use of, the *correct* that explains the intense and sometimes hilarious conservatism of the French when offered combinations of foods to which they are unaccustomed. Mint with lamb is 'bizarre'. But the positive side of *correct* far outweighs its disadvantages. It means one can talk about food, in restaurants or in the home or at the market, assuming a common knowledge and scale of values.

What the English food columns show is that this is not possible here. You can see this when an English reviewer tries to explain why and how a *cassoulet* he has been served was or was not a good one. You can see it in the flowery language that fills the gap left by a lack of reader knowledge. You can see it most clearly in the relentless worship of novelty. What did the food writers say with one voice when the French president criticized English food? We are more 'innovative' than the French. The point is that an ignorant population of eaters treats food like fashion or pop music and demands constant innovation. A culture that already has an excellent cuisine needs no new dishes. It has enough already to fill every day of the year.

An example of misjudged and unnecessary novelty: in a longish column, one well-known English food columnist praises a first course of scallops with black pudding, parsley sauce and creamed potatoes (*Daily Telegraph*, 6 December 2003). Scallops are expensive and make a fine dish. Most people eat them rarely, and for them plain in butter or olive oil would be best. If you must, have a sauce – the French can suggest several. But no one needs scallops, black pudding, sauce and mash, let alone 'to start with'. This is simply unnecessary. I am not blaming the critic or the restaurant. No doubt the ignorant English customers demand such novelties. The widespread existence of these confections – and the endless hunt for new ones – shows not the strength of English food culture but its poverty. The other first course discussed is a 'game' terrine with walnut dressing. The critic is much impressed because the terrine is 'light', though she didn't mind the black pudding clogging up the scallops. It is light because it is made with 'lighter game meats such as rabbit'. Rabbit, of course, is not game. She likes it better than hare, which is 'often too strong'. Hare terrine is one of the great standard French first courses. Is she saying generations of educated French palates are wrong and she is right? Is her palate really so weak that a slice of hare *pâté* is going to stop her tasting the lamb she eats afterwards?

## THE PRICE OF EATING OUT IN ENGLAND

Before we leave the restaurant columnists, there are a few other clues to follow about the state of food in England. The columnists helpfully give the price of eating out. A dinner in London seems to average between £30 and £50 a head with half a bottle of wine. So when the columnist takes his companion the bill could be £100. When a family of four, or two couples, dine out together the damage could be £200. An illuminating article in the *Daily Telegraph* (21 July 2005) took restaurants to task for their prices:

London is

> one of the most expensive places to eat out in the world.

> [D]inner at any premier-league restaurant is going to cost you a minimum of £100 for two, and that doesn't include taxis, tips or the indigestion charge...

> Last night I paid £8.50 for two 0.75 litre bottles of soapy-tasting mineral water...and they weren't even chilled.

You can pay

> £19 for a pasta starter at the Cipriani; or £50 for a main course at Sketch...£8.50 for a pot of tea for one at the Tea Palace; or £40 for a serving of wild salmon at the River Café'.

Neither these nor the average £200 for a family of four are prices many families can afford very often. In summer 2005 several newspapers – including the *Daily Telegraph* (6 August) – reported the results of a survey by the food and grocery think-tank IGD, which found that the £3.5 billion spent on takeaways, restaurants and ready-made sandwiches was the equivalent of £47.57 a month for every man, woman and child. However this sum is made up, once the piles of fast food and sandwiches are deducted, precious little is left for spending on restaurants of any sort, let alone those charging £50 to £100 for two. The £47.57 is, of course, an average. There are people who spend less and a few who spend more. But even the few who spend more do not spend it often. So it is yet more evidence that the restaurant food discussed so colourfully and breathlessly in the weekend supplements is highly unrepresentative of what most English people regularly eat.

## THE COST OF EATING OUT AND EATING AT HOME

It is likewise interesting to compare the cost of eating out in these restaurants with the cost (where appropriate) of eating at home. If the two couples had had the same sort of meal at home, with the same amount of wine, my guess is that it would have been a quarter of the price. It might even have been less. The week in which this was written, Mrs Anderson and I enjoyed a two-and-a-half-pound lobster, preceded by aubergines in oil and followed by salad and cheese, together with a bottle of champagne: just a simple picnic on the beach. It cost under £25. The restaurant price would be over £100. This ratio does not just hold good for good food. I did a study in 2000 on the price of dull food eaten out and eaten in: burgers, omelettes, cups of tea, curries and so on. The ratio is about four to one. Again it can be more, to wit:

*Soup in a café in a shopping centre – £2.90 versus
a tin of supermarket soup heated up at home – 37p:
eating out costs eight times more.*

*A pizza in a pizza place – £5.30 versus a chilled pizza from
the supermarket with three cheeses and tomato heated up
at home – £1.99: eating out costs nearly three times more.*

*A quarter pounder with cheese, no French fries, eaten
out – c. £2 versus a quarter of a pound of minced beef
in a bun with pre-grated/sliced cheese – 70p:
eating out costs around three times more.*

*An old-fashioned meal of two sausages and mash with
onion gravy at a café in a shopping centre – £5.30 versus
two sausages fried at home with mashed potato, milk
and butter or pre-prepared Smash – 50p:
eating out costs almost eleven times more.*

*Sandwiches bought and eaten out in a sandwich joint –
from £1 to £3.50, but average about £1.80 versus two
slices of bread and butter with ham or cheese at home –
under 50p: eating out costs four times more.*

*Tea out – £1.20 versus a tea bag, milk and sugar at home –
4p: eating out costs thirty times more.*

I have a hunch that the 4:1 ratio is a key to what is so
poor about English food. The fact that it is about double the
ratio that is found in France and Spain tells us a lot. The high
cost of consuming dull food out speaks volumes about fixed
costs. The high cost of fancier food tells us that the English
still regard such dining as a 'special occasion' and expect it to
be provided in a special ambience. To be fair, some part of the
explanation is the higher duty payable on wine. But that, too,
reflects a culture that sees wine as a luxury and hence taxable,
rather than part of an ordinary meal. Whatever the details,
there is little in England to compare with a Spanish café used

by local building workers which offers fish soup, small fried hake, salad, bread and wine for the equivalent of £4. It is curious what restaurant columnists do not report. In an earlier chapter I listed the ingredients and dishes that are conspicuous by their absence from domestic British tables. There is a list for restaurants that is just as long. How often on menus do you see pike, herrings, garfish, grey mullet, weever fish, sprats, sea urchins or (Chinese restaurants apart) fresh eel? Why are there so few meat stews? Why is the rare presence of offal always accompanied by jokes or asides about its unusualness? Why are there so few vegetable dishes served in their own right before or after the main course of meat or fish? Why are whole types of meat, mutton and veal so rare?

## DINERS NEED OTHER GOOD DINERS

There's something else missing, too. Some restaurant critics go on about the décor. Some go on about celebrity customers. Occasionally they will tell a tale about awkward customers. What they don't mention is a certain sort of very welcome customer; welcome, that is, to the person who enjoys good food. I can remember eating in a rather ordinary restaurant in Wimereux in the north of France. Near us was a lady of about sixty seated, with her poodle, on a banquette. Both were on the banquette. Both of them looked as if they had just come out of the hairdresser's. The lady wore a frilly blouse and the poodle was sporting a bow. The lady ordered a seafood platter. She sat there slurping oysters, picking meat out of crab claws, chewing on whelks, spitting out the odd operculum she had eaten with a winkle and giving the poodle bits as a treat. It was a pleasure – for us – to see someone eating so efficiently and joyfully. And in France, of course, you can still be surrounded by co-diners all choosing knowledgeably, eating efficiently, and quietly enjoying themselves. Their pleasure is infectious. It is a joy to eat well, surrounded by other people eating well; a joy rarely encountered in England. It is true that standards in Latin countries have declined, in so far as not everyone shops and cooks and eats well. But there are still enough people maintaining their standards. There one shops, cooks and eats *with* a critical mass of other people. Here it is a battle against the ignorant, lazy majority.

I remember a restaurant in southern Italy. Two small boys came in, one about ten years old and his brother – I imagine – about eight. Their father had given them some money to eat out and had 'phoned the restaurant owner to expect them and to take care of them if they became confused or got into difficulties. They needed no help. They clambered up onto chairs facing one another, read through menus, chose with thought but rapidly, waited, chatting happily, and then worked their way through antipasto, pasta, fish, dessert and coffee. Someone had brought them up properly. No one brings children up to eat like that in England. Most English adults do not eat as well as these small children did. Once again, it was a pleasure to be in the same restaurant. Finally, I remember a restaurant in Barcelona. It had no young singles, no young couples, no tourists, no celebrities, no oiks. At each table sat a couple, man and wife, all well into their sixties, exchanging a few words and eating, as the French would say, seriously and correctly. It's a pleasure to eat in such a place. I do not know anywhere like it in England. So I can't blame the restaurant critics for failing to describe clienteles such as these.

Read the restaurant columns carefully and what emerges is a picture of food in England. It is of the fancy restaurant as a place for a special evening out, rather than for a regular weekly dinner. This is why the columnists go on so about the décor and the celebrities. In consequence, the establishments serve special restaurant food and charge special restaurant prices. The food is for exhibition and novelty; it is food the chef knows about and the customer doesn't. It is about showing off. The exhibitionism is contrived, but it fails to hide a widespread lack of familiarity with good food.

### THE POPULAR VERSION OF EATING OUT

The restaurant columns may say a lot about the general culture of food, but they do not describe the restaurants and cafés where most English people eat out most often. To see these it's best to go to a smallish town in the provinces. I live in a village, so to see what is available I chose instead to go to the nearest small to medium town of Bletchley. We start with a simple inventory. Wandering up the main streets I note what's on offer. Will we find here a correctly cooked simple beef *en daube*? Perhaps a traditional beef and kidney pudding in proper suet, a wild duck, eels fried with garlic and parsley, pig's liver in red wine, toad in the hole, stuffed tomatoes, boiled chicken with parsley sauce, soused herrings, boiled ham with pease pudding?

Not exactly. Near the station is a clutch of three restaurants. There is the Golden Curry Balti House, the Rose of India and Wong's House. Down the road, by the high street, there are the Chicken Pizza and Curry House, Veggie World, Tasty Fried Chicken (which announces that it is 'one of the biggest chicken places open in the heart of Bletchley') and Perfect Pizza. At the other end of town – actually in Fenny Stratford – there is the Dinajpur, the Ganges, Aromas Chinese Restaurant, the Napoli Fish Bar and the Bridge. There are also sandwich bars, kebab places, English cafés of the breakfast-all-day type and pubs.

The Bridge does pan-fried garlic mushrooms, chilled honey-dew melon, soup of the day, grilled asparagus, chargrilled steaks, gammon and salmon – that sort of thing. In fact, it is quite a pleasant restaurant. But my guess is that the various restaurants of Bletchley could cope with perhaps 2,000 people in one day. Of those, the Bridge might do a hundred or so. Most of the people who go out in Bletchley do not eat grilled asparagus and gammon. They eat 'Indian' food, Chinese food, fish and chips, café food, kebabs and pizzas. This preponderance is even greater if we note that several of the 'Indian' and Chinese and pizza joints do takeaways: they can cater for far more people than the number of seats they have in the restaurants.

How good are these very popular restaurants, the places that feed the overwhelming majority of English diners out? 'Indians' in England started by providing curries and kormas with rice. There have been waves of change with the arrival of tandoors, Balti cooking and 'sizzling' dishes. Some have tried to offer authentic Pakistani or Bangladeshi food or to special-ize. Some of the Chinese, too, have tried to get away from the European-corrupted Cantonese staples, but without much suc-cess. The food, of course, is as it has to be – fairly instant; dishes are assembled from pre-prepared pastes and cooked meats in the case of the 'Indians', or stir-fried in the case of the Chinese. The menus are enormous. The Golden Curry Balti House offers eleven 'special Balti dishes', three mild Balti dishes, four hot, four dansak Baltis, ten rogan Balti dishes, six vegetarian, six karai dishes, 21 tandoori dishes, 21 curries, five pathia dishes, five dansaks, four masalas, four kormas, four rogans, five dupiazas, four dishes with mushrooms, four with spinach, five with *methi*, four Kashmir, four Malayan, four Bombay, five Special Golden Curry Dishes, four Ceylonese, eleven birianis, fourteen 'special' dishes, 31 side dishes, seven accompaniments and eight breads. Customers are advised to ask about desserts. That's 207 dishes – without the desserts. What it comes down to, of course, is chicken, lamb and prawns as the main ingredients, with rice, bread and vege-tables cooked or re-cooked in four main ways with a variety of pastes and spices.

In fact, the food in Bletchley's several 'Indian' restaurants is quite good. One can eat for about £10 or less. It is freshly prepared or, perhaps one should say, assembled, and is effi-ciently and courteously served. It is not authentic, but no one expects it to be. Some spices and the tomato purée are overdone, but that is how the customers like it. This sort of restaurant clearly fulfils an important function. I'm not sure it does so any better today, despite the additions of Balti, sizzlers and tandoors. For our goal is to establish whether there has been a revolution for the better. As far as 'Indians' are concerned, the reverse is true. Most continue as they have always been. The ones trying to go authentic or to specialize are very much in the minority. And the same may be said of the Chinese. How have the other restaurants done?

The Napoli fish bar is rather good at fish and chips. Better than many others. The key to good fish and chips has always been the same: good potatoes, good fish and oil or, even better, beef fat, which has a high boiling point, plus a skilful staff. Generally speaking, fish and chip shops have deteriorated over the years. Most don't use beef fat or the best oil. Many have branched out into frying all sorts of nonsense, and the principal ingredient, fish, has become, relatively speaking, much more expensive. The customers don't help. They treat the shops mainly as a source of chips, which they like soggy and soaked in ketchup.

The one popular eating place that has, beyond a shadow of doubt, seen a decline in recent years is the café or transport café – at least as far as numbers are concerned. There are far fewer transport cafés than there used to be. Never gourmet establishments, they nevertheless sold a type of food that they did well. Some were renowned for their bubble and squeak, some for their bacon or sausages; others, later in the day, were famous for their liver and onions or pies. As lorries have grown in size and can no longer park in small café car parks, and as motorways have multiplied and taken long-distance drivers off the old main roads where the transport cafés were situated, the cafés have folded. When you do come across one, it is rare to find exceptional quality or character – just more Danish bacon and dull industrial sausages.

If there are fewer cafés, there are far more pizza restaurants and takeaways. If the corrupt version of 'Indian' food sold in UK restaurants can be tolerated, the corrupt version of the pizza cannot. The dough is sometimes not proper bread dough and the base is overloaded with everything but the kitchen sink. Furthermore, unlike the 'Indian', the pizza is not a proper meal. At least those who eat in Indian restaurants sit at table, eat courses, use a knife and fork, engage in conversation and take a little time over lunch or dinner. The pizza, together with the bag or (horrors!) tray of chips and the burger or kebab, is part and parcel of the decline in decent, sociable eating.

## HOW THE ENGLISH EAT THEIR FOOD WHEN THEY ARE OUT

But what, overall, is to be learned about English eating from the observation of popular restaurants? The main lesson is not immediately obvious. The typical dining group at an 'Indian' restaurant starts with a curious confection: a pile of puppadums with two or three sickly sauces, perhaps a sweet chutney, perhaps yoghurt with sugar or honey in. They dollop the sweet rubbish onto the puppadum and wash it down with lager or Chardonnay. Then they have some sort of curry or Balti, usually the same each visit ('I'm going to have my usual vindaloo'). Odd, really, that the restaurants should keep on proudly offering their apparent 207 dishes in the face of such conservatism. And however the restaurant classifies its dishes, the customers do it one way only, by heat ('I can't take a hot one, I'll have chicken korma'). When the meat in sauce arrives with rice, the customers make mud pies, mixing it all up on their plates. Sometimes they push the slop around with naan bread, and the naan they like best is stuffed with something sweet. Chardonnay itself has now become code for sweet. Those diners who like sweetish wine but are aware that it is not considered 'right' can safely order Chardonnay and get the same as they got with German sweetish wine or Mateus Rosé without any loss of face.

When the same people buy their chips they anoint them

with tomato ketchup. This achieves two goals. It makes the chips sweet and, should any chip be so bold as to be crispy, it is immediately rendered soggy. Mushrooms swimming in water and tinned tomatoes do the same at the transport café, and the Chinese are only too happy to make their wares both sweet *and* soggy. The overload on the pizza does the same. And thus, despite the apparent foreignness of curries, pizzas and stir-fries, we find those old English tendencies for soft, sweet mush alive and well. Not even the tiniest revolution in popular eating.

# CHAPTER 7

# HOME COOKING AND THOSE WHO WRITE ABOUT IT

## HOW HOME COOKING IS WRITTEN ABOUT TELLS US A LOT ABOUT THE CULTURE IT IS WRITTEN FOR

Earlier chapters have discussed the extraordinary habits of the Englishwoman (and, less often, the Englishman) in the kitchen and out shopping. This chapter is mostly about what is *written* about cooking at home. Just as we were not directly interested in what restaurant critics wrote, so we are not interested directly in what a few food columnists, cookery book authors and others write about food bought for and prepared at home. Our interest, as always, is in what the vast majority – the readers of the columns and books – know about food, think about food and do with it. And we saw in a few examples showing the laziness of English home cooks in chapter 3 how food writers (unintentionally) reveal the habits of their cook-readers. Food writers, be they restaurant critics or cookery writers, write for an imagined audience. They have readers' letters, surveys and common sense to tell them about the culture of their readers. I am going to presume that, broadly, they know the audience they write for and that what they write reflects various aspects of English food culture. It reflects their readers' knowledge and their culinary concerns. So the question is: what picture of the English home cook can we piece together from the way these food writers write?

## HOME COOKS HAVE ALREADY BEEN TOLD ALL THERE IS TO TELL: THE PROBLEM OF SAYING SOMETHING NEW

No one who knows the least thing about food can be anything but sympathetic to the cookery columnist. I am surprised they have a single hair left on their heads, for there they must be, week after week, scratching their heads to try and come up with something new to say when the best has already been said many times before. Indeed, some of them have themselves said it many times before. Apart from that, there are hundreds of cookery books detailing thousands of dishes, helpfully describing all the processes of roasting, steaming, reducing, pastry-making and stock-making, and listing all the vast battery of instruments that might be used in the kitchen. There are books on the manners of food – most obviously about entertaining. There are books on the sources of food, the countryside and the sea. There are books on the chemistry of food, on food and health, on juggling the demands of the kitchen with a busy life. Besides these books, the thousands of previously written – and we must assume read – columns, and the output of the wireless and the television, there is the knowledge that parents, aunts and friends pass on. So the cookery writer is faced with a readership that has already had explained to it all there is to know.

Moreover, this readership does not need much knowledge because, as I have repeated *ad nauseam*, its members cook less than any former generation (discounting those who had servants to cook for them). The modern home cook cooks properly two or three times a week perhaps, a hundred or so times a year, and she already has access to a wisdom that could inform thousands of meals. Clearly not all home cooks are aware of all this wisdom, though it is difficult to be unaware at least of its existence today on television and in bookshops. If the cookery writer was writing for new cooks – young wives, perhaps – then there would be an opportunity to rerun some of the old material; but all the evidence shows that those who need cookery advice the most, the young and the poor, would rather be sleeping, watching television or staring at mobile 'phones. And some of the columnists have very few of the young and poor among their readership. Consider for a moment the plight of a columnist on a 'quality' newspaper. Her readership is educated, fairly well off, over 25 – just the sort of people who would already have had access to food knowledge. The grammatical tense is important: these people have had the books, have seen the television, have been reading the columns for years. They have already tried out the dishes and incorporated some into their own wisdom. What is the poor columnist to say to them?

## HARPING ON ABOUT THE SEASONS

There are, of course, dodges to jazz up what has been said before. The most glaring and unpersuasive but popular is what might be called the Vivaldi ruse. Its opening lines are 'This is the season for oysters' or 'May is the month for English asparagus' or 'With autumn, the game season arrives' or 'New peas are starting to appear in the shops' or 'Scallops are at their best in February'. After more on the season, it goes on to suggest a few recipes, sometimes even proposing a marriage made in heaven between the oysters and something else also in season. Since meats such as lamb/mutton and game, fish such as crabs, herrings and oysters, and vegetables such as asparagus, peas and beans all have seasons, it is a gambit that can be used often. And it is used often. It is used remorselessly. It can even be turned into a moral argument. For, now that it is politically correct not to import foods because they involve fuel, emissions and the end of the world, using local food becomes virtuous. Local food is often seasonal food, so that becomes virtuous, too. Buying the asparagus in May becomes 'supporting the local community'. For the food columnist searching desperately for topicality, the seasonality of English food is an apparent gift. But it is only apparent, as a closer look at the idea of seasonality shows. The idea is that, for instance, asparagus is in season now, in May, but was not in season in February, March, April, or indeed for nearly a year; so here is something to hail as new.

The trouble is that what at first sight appears to be a gift can be a curse. For asparagus obviously comes into season every year. Far from being new, it *was* in season last May–June, and has been in season every May–June for hundreds of years. It has consequently had lots of past seasons in which to acquire seasonal recipes and comments. There are recipes for asparagus in butter, olive oil, with mayonnaise, various sauces, as a sort of garnish, in soup, in aspics and pastries; these are simple, well-established recipes and are available in countless past publications. Anyone who has been cooking for more than a year will already have had access to all of them. What to do? The columnist can hope the readers *en masse* will succumb annually to short-term memory loss and forget what they knew last year. He can try and persuade the photographer to take up most of the column with a picture so attractive that it will obscure the fact that he has nothing new to say. He can start a bogus controversy about the comparative merits of steaming and boiling. He can discover a disgusting novelty, such as chargrilling asparagus. One or more of these devices might just circumvent his problem for this week, but it only returns next week.

Consider, for instance, a column in *The Times* by Jill Dupleix. It appeared shortly before Christmas 2003, and is about a 'weekend dish', pork and pistachio terrine. The columnist starts off by setting the scene, which is a cocktail party. The guests arrive and, to their joy, find that they don't have to eat the deep-fried won ton or vegetable filo parcels because there is, Miss Dupleix choruses, 'Hallelujah and praise the Lord', a terrine. It is (and recall here the sort of language we found in restaurant columns) 'honest, robust and... hearty'. Hearty *and* robust! Gosh! After a little more of this sort of thing we get the method – mix up the ingredients and put them in a terrine in a *bain marie* – and a list of the ingredients: lean and fat pork, chicken livers, pistachios, spices, herbs, brandy and bacon linings.

It is not that it is a bad or a good recipe. She seems to recommend a ratio of up to 6 parts lean to 1 part fat meat when someone such as Jane Grigson, the author of the standard text (*Charcuterie and French Pork Cookery*, Penguin, 1967) would have recommended a ratio of 1:1 or 1:2, and Miss Dupleix's tablespoonful of minced sage could raise an eyebrow and flatten a taste bud or two. But that is not the point. The point is that this is – the apparent 6:1 apart – a fairly standard *pâté* recipe. Grigson herself, while not giving a recipe with pistachios, mentions their use in various *charcuterie* dishes, so even that is not so new. Why would anyone who was, say, in her thirties and had been cooking for 15 years want another standard *pâté* recipe?

## WHY SHOULD ANYONE WANT ANOTHER RECIPE FOR A DISH FOR WHICH RECIPES HAVE LONG BEEN AVAILABLE?

The question is crucial because it can be asked about almost anything you care to think of: roast lamb, steak, roast pheasant, crab, *aïoli*, *navarin*, salmon in this or that sauce, fishcakes, *lasagne*, mussels. Let me try to answer it. The picture I imagine of *The Times* reader is not entirely correct. She might indeed be fairly well off, over 25 and *generally* educated. She might indeed have once bought, or been given, the half dozen cookery books that are all anyone like her will ever need to fulfil her occasional efforts in the kitchen. But she has not read them. She has not read and annotated them. She has not read, annotated and practised them, and then noted again her own necessary amendments, informed by the experience of her practice. Her copies of the basic cookery books such as Grigson's are not stained red from chicken liver blood, yellow from saffron, and black with squid ink. Their pages are not falling out because they have been used in the kitchen so often that steam has unglued the binding.

## MAGIC IN THE KITCHEN

She did not learn much about food from her mother. Her grandmother did not know a lot either. And she herself was more interested in fashion, sex and music. Not only does she rarely cook, but she has never cooked regularly, and without that discipline she will never cook well. Sometimes people like this buy their cookery books as a sort of magic. They imagine that if they buy the latest, the most acclaimed book, with the most powerful recipes or spells in it, and if they take it into their home and have it near them – as a talisman on a shelf in the drawing room, it will, of itself, throw forth magic rays that will puff up their soufflé, make their mayonnaise 'take' and crisp their pork crackling. But despite the fact that some cookery books actually claim to be 'magic' in their titles, they are not. However good they are, they are worth nothing if the cook is not committed to the work, much of it dull; to the practice and to the cultivation of taste.

I think the same superstition explains why she reads the columns and even cuts them out: 'If I have it, cut it out, make it my own, hold it, pin it to the noticeboard in the kitchen next to the dates of Jemma's riding lessons, it will be an even more powerful ju-ju.' And so it goes on: the poor columnist providing more of the same, the reader hoping that this time, the 'right' spell or recipe will do the trick. In the Dupleix column, there is one little piece that deserves notice and supports, surely unintentionally, this picture of the reader as generally educated but a hopeless cook. She advises the reader to slice the terrine thickly on a large white plate. She further suggests offering the terrine on a plate with a sharp knife. Is the reader so incompetent that she cannot work out for herself the suitable thickness of slices, the size of plate and the superiority of a sharp knife over a blunt one? Probably she really is just that incompetent.

## THE ENGLISH COOK AND WILD ANIMALS

Take a couple of recipes, both for pheasant. The first is not really a recipe, more of a recommendation from Rita Exner (*The Times*, Body and Soul, 3 September 2005). She kicks off with classic Vivaldi: 'The game season now includes partridge [did it ever not?]...or try pheasant, for a flavoursome change, using your favourite poultry recipe to roast or casserole. Its flavour is similar to free-range chicken or turkey and you get a wonderful gravy.' Pheasant does not taste similar to chicken, any more than beef tastes similar to lamb; and, moreover, chicken does not taste similar to turkey. Of course, if they did all taste similar, as Miss Exner mistakenly supposes, then there would be no point in having pheasant 'for a flavoursome change' since it wouldn't be a change. But once again, it is not the columnist's odd remarks that are interesting but the readers' reactions. One can get away with remarks like this because the readers have no informed food culture. I sometimes think one could list ground glass as an essential ingredient in stews and get no reaction (or any fatalities!).

This is not an isolated example. Miss Exner is not a celebrity. Gordon Ramsay is. Writing on hare in ale with saffron in *The Times* Magazine (10 September 2005), he says: 'If you are unable to find hare, then you can replace it with two jointed rabbits.' To be sure you *can* replace hare with rabbit, but it will not taste at all similar: hare is hung and is game meat; rabbits should be paunched immediately they are shot and are not game.

Then there is Rowley Leigh in the *Sunday Telegraph*. He is going to cook *salmis* of pheasant. And why not? The recipe is fine – up to a point, or rather back to a point. Like so many recipes, it starts at the point where the pheasants are sitting in the fridge. The interesting part – the part good cooks need to know about before they get to a recipe – is what happened before the pheasants ended up in the fridge. Pheasants are wild animals; or, more correctly, they are domestically reared animals that have been helped to become wild. Wild animals present a peculiar problem in that they vary. They vary in age most obviously: pheasants released from pens in September and shot in October will be different from those shot in January, and from those that survive over the next year and are shot in subsequent seasons. The cocks, too, are bigger and tougher than the hens. Pheasants that have been properly hung for a couple of weeks will be more tender and will taste different from those eaten fresh. That is presumably why Mr Leigh uses breasts and thighs but sets aside the drumsticks for stock. I think he should explain this. He should explain that the drumsticks may or may not have sinews. If the birds have been properly butchered then their sinews will have been drawn (the butcher or cook makes an incision round the skin at the 'knee', without cutting the sinew itself, then pulls the sinews out; the same procedure applies, by the way, to ducks, geese, chickens and any robust bird). But many people do not bother with this; they are lazy and wrong.

The long and the short of it is this. Ingredients such as pheasants are best encountered as early as possible, so the cook can know something of their age and history, how long they have been hung, etc. He can, of course, rely on others to know – and to pass the information on – but others are increasingly unreliable. If a pheasant is presented plucked, drawn, with its feet chopped off and its spurs consequently missing then, unless the information is passed along, the cook will be cooking by guesswork. Readers who are to cook pheasant need to be told how to find them, how to hang, pluck and clean them, and how to draw out their sinews. That is far more important than knowing a new recipe.

### THE GOOD COOK GOES BACK AS FAR AS POSSIBLE IN THE SUPPLY CHAIN

It would not matter, this business of source knowledge and going back to the earliest point, if it only applied to pheasants;

but it applies to nearly all wild animals, including hares. It is most important to know whether your hare is last season's leveret, and thus fairly tender, or is elderly and tough. How long has it been hung? When the weather is cold it will benefit from three weeks' hanging. If the butcher butchers it, has he kept the blood that has collected in the thorax? Hares can be eaten young or old, hung or fresh, with or without blood, clean shot or shot up, but you have to know in order to cook them appropriately. Most cookery columnists rarely write about this. A pity. The point about knowledge and wild food includes certain fish, too. Everyone knows that shellfish should be fresh. What they are not told loudly enough is that crabs, lobsters, clams, scallops and eels should be bought live and killed and cooked *at the last moment*. This presents no difficulty when it comes to clams, which are simply opened in wine or whatever; but eels have to be grabbed squirming, their heads cut off and their guts taken out while they are still bending. Scallops have to be cleaned. Cooks should know how to sex crabs and discern how full they are before buying them. This is part of what is involved in being a cook. And it is a part the cookery writers largely and prudently avoid, because this crucial part of cooking is hard work and messy work. So is cleaning raw sheep's tripe or taking the meat off a pig's head or making *boudin* with blood.

## COOKING FROM SCRATCH

There is a little phrase that Mr Ramsay uses about the hare or rabbit: 'Ask your butcher to skin and joint it for you.' This occurs frequently in other columnists' advice, as in: 'Ask your fishmonger to clean the scallops.' How charming is that word 'your', as if the readers all had personal butchers or fishmongers. How reckless to trust most of the people who sell fish to do any such thing. The only way you know it has been done properly – in England – is to do it yourself. And doing it yourself helps the cook understand the later processes of cooking.

Indeed, he or she starts to cook in an entirely different way. Instead of deciding what dish he is going to serve and then demanding that the ingredients fit the bill, he starts at the beginning, goes to the butcher, sees what is best, brings it home, studies it and only then decides which way of cooking it will be the most suitable.

Sometimes he will be able to decide at the butcher's or fishmonger's. He will look at the squid and, if it is Californian ex-frozen, he will know that he cannot fry it because it will steam in the gallons of water it will release. He will see that, although the monk is fresh, it is being sold without the head because the wholesaler is concerned about transport costs and he knows his customers are so useless at food that none would be prepared to pay for heads (the head is required to make the stock to mix with the *aïoli*), so no *bourride* tonight. On the other hand there are some crippled lobsters going cheap because the punters mistakenly think the claw is the best meat (it is, of course, the head).

Sometimes the cook will, when he gets his pheasants home and has a good look at them, find that one has been rather shot up and should not be hung; or when he tries to crack his rabbit's jaw, it takes a lot of pressure, indicating that the rabbit is old, will be tough and should not be roasted. So instead he might stew it with lentils. Cooking, then, is improvising with ingredients according to principles, matching methods and recipes to ingredients once one has found out exactly what these particular ingredients are like. It is not setting out with a wish list and trying to make the actual daily reality of fish and meat fit some plan suggested by a column or book.

### LACK OF MORAL COMMITMENT

Faced with this definition of cooking, what is the recipe writer to do? The best thing would be to abandon the recipe format altogether and use the space to instruct the lazy, squeamish English cook in the unpleasant facts of life. But the readers do not want to get their hands dirty, continually adjust their plans, or spend time plucking, disembowelling, scaling and filleting. The failure of the English home cook is essentially moral. She is not prepared to commit herself to the daily demands of good cooking. The women's magazines know well the limits of their cook-readers' commitment. One suggests that cooks 'in a hurry' should use pre-prepared vegetables. These daunting vegetables turn out to be a couple each of onions, carrots and courgettes. It would take a minute to slice them, but a minute the modern English woman will not spend. Another suggests using 'ready sliced and ready grated cheddar cheese' for a 'brilliantly easy topping'. So careless of the welfare and contentment of her family and friends is the modern lady that grating her own cheese is too much effort. The magazines and the columns have to collude in this moral failure. No fault may be found with the modern lady. Thus there is a column that suggests an oven-baked dish should be abandoned and left to another day if the weather turns out to be good and the cook might get too hot in the kitchen. Another suggests doing a weekly market shop, despite the fact that many of the items needed, such as fish and poultry, should be bought the same day as they are cooked. Many a column extols the 'easy', the 'quick' and the 'trouble-free' as manifest virtues. Very few warn that hard work is necessary, and not one that I have read insists on practising a dish before inflicting it on others.

This moral failure has not lessened in the course of the alleged revolution in English food. It has deepened. The contemporary middle-aged cook cooks less than a quarter of the number of meals her mother did. She cooks proper meals less and less frequently. She relies more and more on pre-prepared food. She knows less and less about its sources. She wants cooking to be quick, undemanding, even to be 'fun'. Not only has the cooking got worse, but it will get even worse yet. The new generation of home cooks are even lazier and less committed than their mothers. A survey of 18 to 35-year-olds found half could not even make a green salad. The survey, done by the food store Cranks and reported in the *Daily Telegraph* (20 August 2005), found that young people typically spend less than ten minutes preparing a meal by opening a packet or putting something in a microwave. Ben Johnson of Cranks is reported as saying that the vast majority of them believe that many dishes are too complicated to prepare. The young people themselves, of course, admitted to no such failing. They were short of time, lacked knowledge and preferred 'convenience'.

## KITCHEN EQUIPMENT AS A JU-JU

Without moral commitment it would need a miracle for the occasional, paltry efforts made in the kitchen by the young or middle aged to result in a good meal. So it is a miracle that the modern home cook demands. And the cookery book or column is the spell she foolishly supposes will work the miracle. When one spell fails, she demands another. Spells are not the only ju-ju she tries in her attempt to conjure good food from her incompetence and lack of commitment. There is another sort of food writing that casts some light on these food spells. It is to be found in the advertisements for kitchen equipment. If a recipe spell fails to redeem poor cooking, then perhaps a gadget might work ('Perhaps my omelette will be fluffier if I keep my eggs "cool and fresh" in a terracotta egg store'). In just a few pages of one gadgets magazine we find the following gifts and 'essentials': a British-made 'blanket to keep plates hot', a tea-bag tin, the Keep-Warm Toaster, a stainless steel top trolley, a herb keeper, heat-resistant spatulas, a microwave double steamer, a tool with which one can 'drain and serve single-handed' and a chef's hat and apron with 'The finishing touch – the owner's name, or perhaps that of their favourite TV chef, authentically embroidered in script on both (up to twelve letters).'

These rather naff and lower middle-class ju-jus are easy to laugh at, though they are widely bought. But the bigger and more expensive ju-jus bought by wealthier and more educated people are even more pathetic. Surpassing all in idolatry is the belief that spending £5,000 on a new kitchen will appease the gods and make dinner parties the talk of suburbia. People seem willing to endure weeks of dust and disorder, spend wads of money on the kitchen and then more on a new cooker to make a miracle happen. The truth is that most cooks need no more than a simple four-ring cooker, a fridge, a table, one sink and a dresser, all in a small room.

## THE CHALLENGE OF CHRISTMAS

There is one time of year when all this sorcery, incompetence and self-deception unites with some of the other evil tendencies in English cooking discussed elsewhere in this book (such as the love of a hundred and one vegetables cooked badly, rather than one cooked well or Special Occasionism) in an explosion of bad food – Christmas. Only one thing is worse than the food served on Christmas Day, and that is the food served in the week that follows. Once again the *writing* about food offers some clues. The dominant theme in the columns that appear before Christmas is what a daunting challenge Christmas cooking is. As Xanthe Clay put it for the *Daily Telegraph* (6 December 2003), the problem is 'how to produce sumptuous food without suffering a nervous breakdown'. Another columnist talks of the need for 'military planning'. Such planning harks back to the days when newspapers offered cooks a three-week countdown chart of the tasks necessary to produce one – usually rather bad – Christmas meal. Yet another columnist, the chef Gordon Ramsay, raises the prospect of failure: 'the turkey's raw, the carrots have disintegrated and nobody is speaking to the dog because it has eaten the sausages'. He wants to make 'double sure there are no hitches on the day' (*The Times* Magazine, 6 December 2003).

The ominous 'day' captures it all. What is the poor cook to do when faced with the awful challenge of 'the day'? And how can the columnist help?

In fact, there is nothing extraordinary about Christmas. It is simply another season. The English are unnaturally but firmly attached to the turkey, excessive numbers of vegetables, including the obligatory sprouts, and superfluous 'trimmings' – overcooked Danish bacon, nasty chipolatas, silly stuffings and sauces, the whole lot swamped in industrial gravy. The more adventurous cooks experiment with organic turkeys, ham, or a goose and make their own gravy by reducing the filth at the bottom of the roasting pan using Australian wine. But, basically, the show is the same every year. That, of course, should make it easy. All you have to do is learn to do it once, get it right, make a note of what you did, then do the same every year. The cook might need the help of a columnist once to get it right initially, though it's all in the books. Anyway, all that is involved is roasting and boiling. What is all the fuss about?

In fact, it gets easier with every passing year because, following the triumph of moral relativism and decadence, the English family gets smaller every year and its religious and traditional obligations become non-existent. It used to be daunting to have to feed four children, four grandparents, a husband, two lonely neighbours, an aunt or two and oneself, go to Mass, take part in traditional pastimes and games, and dress for the various occasions. But today's family is a lone parent with a child who may or may not turn up for dinner. There are no competing activities except binge drinking and television, and no formal requirements. Where's the challenge in that? Yet there is no doubt that people get in a fuss and that, as Mr Ramsay rightly warns, failure is possible. Indeed, in my experience, failure is the norm.

This is hardly surprising, for the English Christmas dinner has all the ingredients of culinary disaster. Just consider the

Christmas dinner for the slightly larger family. Its ingredients include one mother who rarely cooks and is therefore unpractised and incompetent. She may also resent having to cook. There is a 'partner' who may well turn up late for lunch and drunk. There are two sons who are already bored with Christmas and an old family friend who tries to help with the carving because the cook can't carve and the drunk partner is not to be trusted. Anyway, the knife is not sharp – it never is – and there is neither a steel nor anyone who would know how to use one – there never is. Whether the family does actually expect a traditional lunch or not I have no idea, but somehow everyone feels that everyone else expects it. This means cooking at least six vegetables, of which two must be potatoes and sprouts, plus the 'trimmings' and bird, together with any other courses. The cook needs to cope with a dozen items, each of which has a different cooking time, and to coordinate their preparation so that they are ready together at the appointed time. That is difficult for an unpractised cook. Why should it be necessary? It is monstrous bad taste to want more than two vegetables. Vegetables, as we have said elsewhere, are best cooked as dishes in their own right and served before or after the meat. If it is felt the goose needs something, a few white beans with onions are quite enough. Why not serve the turkey with a proper bubble and squeak of sprout tops and potatoes? Just that. Why have turkey anyway? It once had the supposed advantage – over goose – that it could feed many, but there are no longer many to be fed.

### FOOD COLUMNISTS TO THE RESCUE

And what do the columnists advise? They say the same every year, but limply try to make it sound new. This is either a variation on 'do as much as you can in advance' (what? – start the day before, or set the turkey going in a slow oven in September?) or 'keep it simple'. The advance business doesn't work. It actually involves the incompetent cook in more cooking, and cooking, after all, is what she cannot do. Simplification is not right either. It is not that the cooking is intrinsically difficult but that the expectations are gross (and tasteless) and the cook not up to them. Perhaps the correct word is not 'simple' but 'appropriate'. It would, I suppose, be possible to find a dish 'appropriate' to the meagre skills of the cook, but to mention it would offend not only her but the expectations of others for 'the day'.

The task of the food columnist, at least in the mind of the newspaper editor who pays him or her, is to please the readers, not to insult them. Yet an accurate explanation of what is wrong with English cooking at Christmas (and every day) would involve some very harsh words indeed. No large-circulation newspaper will print those words. Christmas demonstrates just how bad English food still is. Indeed, given the increase in disposable income and the reduction in the number of people to be fed, it can fairly be judged to have got worse. Once again, any 'revolution' that has occurred has been for the worse. The food columns, while they can help to show just how bad the food is, are largely irrelevant to its ever getting better. They present the problem of Christmas, or indeed of any meal, as being technical or organizational, whereas it is actually moral.

CHAPTER 8

# FOOD IN HOSPITALS AND SCHOOLS, ON PLANES AND PICNICS

## THE ENGLISH EAT A LOT OF THEIR FOOD NEITHER IN RESTAURANTS NOR AT HOME

To get some idea of how well, or how badly, the English eat we have to consider the many places in which they eat. It is difficult to know what proportion of their eating is done at home. It is much higher, of course, than the eating they do in restaurants. Once upon a time, when few of them went out to work, most Englishwomen ate almost entirely at home. Their children ate at home and at school. Their husbands ate at the works canteen and at home. Now that more women go out to work, they and their husbands eat their midday meal neither at home, nor in works canteens. Instead they lunch on what they buy in sandwich shops or from the food counters of bigger stores, and in takeaways; or they might pop into cafés, cheap restaurants or pubs near their work. Many children do not eat school lunches but rather browse on a mixture of food taken from home and bought in takeaways, chip shops, vending machines and sweet shops.

In addition, hospital patients eat hospital food; prisoners eat prison food; travellers eat airport food, airline food, motorway service station food, car ferry food, transport café food, railway station food and food bought on trains. We should add to this food served in (gentlemen's) clubs, eaten on picnics, bought while shopping or in stores with cafés, and sold in hotels.

Some of this food is bought and eaten in the same place – for instance, in the case of the hotel. Some is bought from shops or takeaways and then eaten in the street, parks or car parks; in cars; off desks at the office; while sitting, standing, walking, working or reading. This is not important for our purposes, except that, if we are talking about the *quality* of food in England today, about the *quality* of eating, then this solitary consumption of food, not at table but while engaged in some other activity, can scarcely be seen as an improvement. What about the quality of the food itself? We have already seen that those who congratulate England on vastly improving its food base their claim largely on a tiny number of expensive restaurants that most English people never patronize. The other, cheaper, restaurants and home food show no sign of a revolution in quality – at least not for the better. And nor do the other places just mentioned, with the possible exception of sandwich bars.

## AIRLINE FOOD

Let's start with airline food. The cooked food that airlines serve is pretty horrid: tiny portions of tasteless chicken or beef in shiny gravy with three cubes of greasy potato and a sprig of chewy broccoli. No person of taste in his right mind would bother to eat this. Rather, he would prepare a modest picnic. He would take one of those thin waxed carrier bags you get from confectionery shops. At the bottom might go an aluminium foil container with some ripened, unpasteurized *Camembert* and *Gorgonzola*, with a few grapes and a stick of celery. In the next container up could be a roast partridge with some *frisée*. The top carton might have a dressed crab with a few olives. The picnic would be completed by some bread in a plastic bag, pepper ground just before leaving the house, a lemon, any other condiments and – most important – a damask table napkin, without ring. Quail, pheasant or half a (domestic) duck might replace the partridge. Lumpfish caviar or half a lobster or a salad of potato and anchovies could provide an alternative to the crab. In the past I have taken oysters, but the airline crew has never had a suitable knife with which to open them and one is currently forbidden to take one's own.

The drill is simple. On a flight, say, to New York from Heathrow leaving at 9.00 am, spend the first two or three hours working or reading. Refuse all drinks and food offered by the staff. After two or three hours all the other passengers will have eaten the airline food, had a drink and been served coffee. The food and hot liquid then propel them all to use the lavatories at the same time. More accurately, it makes them wish to use the lavatory at the same time. But they have to queue. You can ignore all that. Soon the scrum is over and they, having eaten rubbish food for the masses, settle down to watch rubbish films for the masses. The sensible diner then calls the steward and buys two splits of champagne. These disposed of, he asks for a tiny bottle of white or red (carefully avoiding anything called Chardonnay or from Australia) and a knife and fork. He doesn't bother with the napkin. It's paper and will go to pieces in the face of the lemon juice. He takes his own napkin, puts it on his tray with his bread and condiments and the top container – the crab. After that, and having switched from white to red, he eats the partridge, and then rounds the picnic off with the cheese. It is not, to be sure, a proper meal, but then light meals are best when flying. Eating like this has many advantages, quite apart from enjoyment of the meal itself – there is the delicious anticipation of it while one is working or reading and while one is sipping the champagne. One can eat it slowly, savouring it, and thus using up time. Afterwards, the food and the wine together are just enough to induce a couple of hours of very pleasant siesta. One wakes up just in time to refuse the ice-cold sandwiches offered by the crew shortly before arrival in New York.

I have enjoyed some excellent meals and flights this way and always recommend it, even when travelling Business

Class. The same obviously goes for long-distance trains such as Eurostar. On coming back from New York, one may not have a domestic kitchen to prepare the picnic in. However, a visit to Little Italy will furnish a pleasant light lunch of artichokes in olive oil, mortadella, Parma ham and salami with olives, followed by a green salad and some goat's cheese. Should you be more than usually misanthropic, you could call at some of the excellent Pakistani cafés around 29th, between 3rd and Park, and choose a selection of brains *masala*, *paya* (sheep's feet) and *chana*.

## WHY THE ENGLISH WILLINGLY ACCEPT THIRD-RATE FOOD

This solution to airline eating is obvious and does not take much effort. The fact that hardly any English passengers do anything like it, and instead put up with the horrid food offered, shows just how wet and useless their food culture is. And not just their food culture. Watch them drinking – or rather not drinking. Twenty years ago airlines pressed drink on passengers. The trolleys went ceaselessly up and down the aisles and everyone drank more than they would normally. Now new health fads predominate, and one has to ask for drink – sometimes ask repeatedly. English travellers obediently drank all they were offered twenty years ago and now obediently hardly drink anything. Anyone of taste would, of course, drink what he was used to – the quantity he wished to – neither augmenting nor reducing it in obedience to current nonsense codes. But these people have no taste – that they are prepared to stand up for.

## PICNICS ARE THE ANSWER TO SO MANY PROBLEMS

The airline example is enlightening in another way. What the sensible person eats is a picnic. There are lots of places you can eat a picnic: in planes, trains, stations, airports, in one's bedroom when marooned on some ghastly residential management training weekend...But English people will only eat

picnics out of doors. Why I don't know, except they have the food imagination of sheep.

When they do have picnics in parks and fields, on race-courses and beaches, they eat the dullest food imaginable: boring sandwiches, crisps, the occasional cold industrial sausage or ham or a soggy rice salad. This is usually made even worse by the addition of takeaway food of chips and burgers. The French or Spanish on a picnic will have whole dishes: a cold roast duck, an omelette, a whole salmon, *pâté*. The lunch is properly eaten in courses with everyone eating the same thing at the same time; not, as in England, a sort of grab-it-yourself buffet. In particular, the Spanish are likely to take a double-circled gas ring wide enough to cook *paella* or some other dish. That transforms picnics, making it possible to cook and eat most things one could cook on a flame at home.

## FOOD IN HOSPITALS AND SCHOOLS

Wherever you find the English eating, you will find them eating badly. It is really very odd the way that the same newspapers which announce the great revolution for the better in English food fail to see this. In fact, they are part of the depraved food culture themselves, only looking for good food in restaurants, and not on picnics or in aeroplanes. They should be aware of just how bad the food is since, having praised 'London food' on one page, they then work themselves up into a panic about the national junk diet on the next. This junk diet is what is consumed at home or bought from take-aways and cheaper restaurants. In the last two years they have also discovered that English schoolchildren eat so badly that they may be harming themselves, and that the self-congratulating National Health Service inflicts on the sick and the dying some of the worst food in the country. It is routine for patients to leave hospital worse nourished than when they were admitted. Both the state schooling system and the state hospital system are vast. Taken together, their appalling standards affect millions of people – far more than expensive restaurants. It is curious, too, that the same nanny state that daily reprimands mothers for feeding children badly at home and scolds food producers and retailers for persuading children to eat sweets and crisps should use its own monopoly power – a power far greater than theirs – to inflict disgusting meals on the public. Thus Barbara Lantin, writing in the *Daily Telegraph* (16 March 2005) reports what a physiotherapist was given to eat on the evening of her admission to a North London teaching hospital: 'There was no food for me. Eventually they sent me some revolting dried-up cod…The food was just as awful on other days – badly cooked and tasteless…The meals were…scarcely edible.' Lantin quotes Rick Wilson of the British Dietetic Association, a dietician at King's College Hospital, London, who says that service can be 'appalling'. What he has in mind, she says, is that food is served while patients are asleep or away from the ward. It is not just a matter of the odd anecdote. Some 40 per cent of hospital food is wasted. (For 'wasted' read 'not eaten'.) Of that 40 per cent more than a quarter goes untouched, that is 17 million meals; 55,000 meals are thrown away each day; 60 per cent of hospital patients are malnourished.

The school food problem is slightly different. It has come onto the agenda because the healthy-eating lobby finds the food children choose unhealthy, with too many sweets and crisps and not enough fruit and vegetables. Apparently three-quarters of school lunch boxes fail to meet the basic nutritional standards, as children continue to favour crisps, chocolate and fizzy drinks over fruit and vegetables (*The Times*, 1 September 2004). More than 50 million lunch boxes are made each year, and the favourite is still white bread sandwich, crisps and a chocolate bar or cake. It is not only that these children are given poor food by their schools and parents; their parents fail to teach them about food and they become incompetent as young adults. Some 48 per cent of 18 to

35-year-olds do not know how to make a simple green salad (*Daily Telegraph*, 20 August 2005). They typically do not spend any more than ten minutes preparing any meal. Having left school and gone (as all young people are persuaded they must) to university, as students they eat even worse, with some consuming toast and economy cheese for up to a week on end when the money runs out.

But we are getting sidetracked: our concern is with the quality of food as food, not as a health issue. The diet demanded by the health freaks is itself pretty miserable, and one can understand why the children – and especially the young people given their freedom at university – reject it. But why do they choose crisps and sweets, and why do their parents supply them? Even more important, why do they like poor food? No one emerges from this business looking good. Why, for example, do our children reject food that French or Italian children relish? There are currently attempts to suggest that dislike of certain foods has a biological cause. Apparently, 25 per cent of the population are 'supertasters', people with more taste buds than average on the tongue. These people have stronger food dislikes and retain relics of an earlier evolutionary distaste for bitter foods. Such explanations are next to useless. Presumably there are French and Italian children who are 'supertasters', too, but still they eat their spinach and demand more.

## THE FOOD PROBLEM IS CULTURAL, NOT INFORMATIONAL OR FINANCIAL

The currently fashionable way of dealing with the ghastly food eaten by schoolchildren and served to hospital patients is to blame expenditure and training. Give more money for use in school and hospital catering, train the staff better, conduct awareness campaigns to educate parents and children and all will be well. This is nonsense because it fails to recognize the problem for what it is. The truth is that the vast majority of parents, children and school and hospital staff do not know what good food is. The problem is a cultural one and one of comparatively long standing. The bad food in schools and hospitals is merely one consequence of being part of a society with an impoverished food culture. Even when money is plentiful the English will eat badly. Shoppers in shopping malls are not starved of 'financial resources' but they buy trash food. Families out for picnics in the country or on the beach at weekends are not cash poor but they prepare and take and eat third-rate food. Families going on holiday on cross-Channel ferries have their pockets and handbags stuffed with sterling, euros and plastic but they buy and eat bad food. To be more precise, they buy, eat and leave bad food.

I have already mentioned the behaviour of the masses on a cross-Channel ferry. The first thing they do on board is to make for the restaurants and form a long queue. Why? There's no hurry. They have at least an hour and a quarter in which to eat, and anyway they can generally concentrate on their food for only 10 minutes before they are attracted to some other form of entertainment. So why the rush? Is it because they are starving? How could they be? Surely they organized a good breakfast before they left home or took a carefully assembled picnic to eat in the car on the way to Dover? Of course they didn't! Too lazy and too ill organized. Indeed, too much money rather than too little is probably the problem.

### AND FOOD ON THE BEACH

For a final tale of horror, we return to the beach. Late last summer I was on a beach in England. Near me was a middle-class English family, with two girls in their pre-teens, a mother, a grandmother and a grandfather. It was one o'clock. They had been eating intermittently throughout the morning and were to continue eating throughout the afternoon. Like many other people on the beach, they chewed slices of pizza and bacon and cheese puffs that they had bought ready made at a shop on the way to the beach. Mum had brought a huge sack with individual bags of crisps. These were dipped in industrial mayonnaise. Occasionally, children were sent off to buy industrial ice creams with brightly coloured things in them. Various adults would disappear and return with boxes of soggy chips smothered in tomato ketchup, then disappear again to buy hamburgers – with more ketchup. Everything else was eaten with fingers, but for some unfathomable reason the chips were stabbed in a 'refined' manner with a short wooden fork, which the stabber had to grip in such a way that the thumb became soaked in ketchup and blobs of soggy chip. In between there were bars of milk chocolate, chewing gum, fried chicken nuggets and all manner of brightly coloured fizzy drinks, together with the occasional lager for the adults. Grandfather spent much of the morning eating cold, fat encrusted chipolatas.

At one o'clock he announced his intention of taking the girls to the top of the cliff to the promenade, where he would buy them (another) ice cream and where they could hear a band play. Mother said, 'Alright, in a while, but they've got to have lunch first.' Grandfather looked puzzled, 'But we've had lunch.' 'Of course we haven't', insisted Mother. 'Yes we have.' 'No, we haven't.'

Who was right? *Had* they had lunch? How would they know if they had had lunch? Once upon a time you knew when you had had lunch, and indeed when you were having it, because it was a much bigger meal than elevenses, the first meal since breakfast, and you ate different food at lunch from that eaten as snacks. But now the same sort of food in the same sorts of quantities is eaten throughout the day. How would one know which of these identical snacks was 'lunch'?

Of course, the grandfather and the mother were both wrong. These and vast numbers of 'families' (the word needs some analysis: most are not complete families in the traditional sense) no longer have lunch or breakfast or dinner. Indeed, they would not even know what lunch was. What an achievement – to have got rid of proper meals and proper food entirely, together with the knowledge of what they are. It is not that the English eat better or worse meals than they used to. They are not up to eating meals at all – or even to agreeing what they consist of. What a revolution in English food! After – well, I *was* going to say 'lunch' but I'd better say each instalment of food, one member of the fractured family dutifully took a pile of the polystyrene dishes to throw away in the litter bin. A casual inspection revealed that the dishes had enough chips and ketchup still on them to feed Somalia.

## CHAPTER 9

# FOOD IDEOLOGUES AND ASSORTED NUTTERS

### HEALTHISTS

The way English people buy, prepare and eat food is currently under the influence of an assortment of ideologues, many of whom would, in wiser years, have been ignored and derided as nutters. There are healthists, people convinced that the minutiae of diet have substantial effects on health – and that they have been entrusted with the secrets of a healthy diet. It should be remembered that, even in its weakest and most general formulation, their claim is new and controversial. People across the globe eat very different diets, and it has long been recognized that human beings can prosper on a variety of diets, so long as they have enough food and certain essentials. The healthists, however, propound one official diet for all, wherever they may be, be they rich or be they poor, elderly or adolescent, strong or frail, irrespective of the diseases and infirmities they may suffer from. Other scientists and experts who question this one diet are dismissed as outdated or *parti pris*. For this reason the healthists should be regarded as ideologues.

The healthists are reductionists. When they look at a fresh egg, perfectly boiled, salted and peppered, gleaming yellowy-orange with a soldier of buttered toast, they don't see an egg and soldier; they don't imagine the glorious taste and salivate like normal people. Instead, they see fat, salt, cholesterol and refined starches. And what do they feel? Not hunger but fear. They tremble for their own longevity, though why they should wish to extend their pleasureless lives is beyond me. Then they feel an uncontrollable urge to interfere with other people's boiled eggs and pleasure; to warn, scare, urge, campaign, nag and control.

Related to the healthists, but distinct from them, are the food safety people. They are the ones that worry about salmonella and listeria. When they see a 'boily', they see diarrhoea, fever and death. It is they who were responsible for closing down Britain's small slaughterhouses and depriving good cooks of the wherewithal to make and eat tripe, brains and sweetbreads. It is they who drove countless small egg producers out of business. If that 'boily' tastes bland and boring, blame them. It is they who continually threaten live (unpasteurized) cheese. Together with their health-and-safety chums here and in Brussels, they dream up the regulations that do so much damage to good food.

## THE GREAT VEGETARIAN LIE

Then there are the vegetarians, of whom there are three sorts. Some won't eat any meat. Some won't eat any meat or fish. Some won't eat meat unless it's chicken or is covered in sauce so that it doesn't look as though it's come from any animal (or unless it's the weekend). Many are barmy. Most are ill-mannered: they demand special diets when they come to eat with normal people, but never give normal people meat when they do the entertaining. But the most important thing about vegetarians is that they lie about the joys of a vegetarian diet. The best cuisines of the West, especially of bourgeois and regional France, centre on meat and fish. Of course they use vegetables, but the main dish is nearly always fish or meat, and indeed the main dishes are sometimes *only* fish and meat. It is meat that provides the stocks and some of the fats, the basis of pastries, the *charcuterie* and the extremities for some of the best first courses. You cannot eat this cuisine in a vegetarian way. It is simply not true to say that a vegetarian meal is as good, as enjoyable, as a traditional French dinner. Matters are even worse with much Spanish food since it often mixes meat and vegetables or fish and vegetables. Take away the meat and fish and you not only lose the meat and fish dishes, you lose the best vegetable dishes as well. Those chickpeas just don't taste the same without the finely chopped *jamon* or *chorizo* or *morcilla*. Vegetarian food may be healthy. It may benefit animals. But it is a lie to suggest that it tastes as good as proper food. The matter of lying and vegetarianism is an interesting one. A survey by Taylor Nelson AGB (reported in the *Spectator*, 4 October 1997) found that while 7 per cent of Britons describe themselves as vegetarians, only 4 per cent eat a meat-free diet. Put another way, nearly half of vegetarians are liars. It does not explain whether they are liars because they are vegetarians, or whether there is something about lentils and brown bread that attracts untruthful people. But obviously vegetarians should not trust other 'vegetarians'. Whether they lie to each other is of no concern to sensible eaters, of course, but they shouldn't lie to us. Their Great Lie is, as mentioned before, that their diet is as fine as other diets, such as French classic cuisine. This is simply not true, and it is an interesting lie because, as we shall see, it is essentially the same lie as that told by food healthists.

Furthermore, in practice many vegetarians turn out to be people who don't really care about food. This is convenient for them, stuck as they are with their awful diet. But it makes matters even worse when they do try to cook and entertain 'us', people used to good food and who value it. And another thing. Writers as perceptive as Orwell and Buchan have remarked that people who are nutty about food are, not infrequently, nutty about other things as well, such as politics, art or morality. Eat with vegetarians and not only do you get second-rate food, cooked by people whose heart is not in it and who have no manners, but they will regale you with diatribes about patriarchy or capitalism to go with your sloshy lentils.

HEATH

## ORIGINS OF FOOD IDEOLOGUES AND NUTTERS

There are other ideologues and nutters, anti-alcohol crusaders, environmentalists, supplement enthusiasts and the get-thin industry. England increasingly resounds to the shouts of this assortment: eat lots of fruit; no, don't eat fruit if it comes across the globe and causes pollution; yes, do eat it if it comes across the globe from poor countries; no, don't eat foreign fruit, support English fruit and vegetables; eat organic meat; don't eat any meat; eat lots of fish for your e-oils; don't eat too much fish because of the dioxins; don't eat any fish in short supply; don't eat any fish full stop – sprats have feelings just like you and me.

This obsession with not eating this and not eating that is comparatively new and it is peculiar to certain countries. As I have said, traditionally the concern about food has been to have enough of it to stave off starvation, and enough of the essentials to avoid malnutrition.

In his book *The Death of Humane Medicine* (Social Affairs Unit, 1995), Petr Skrabanek finds various examples of dietary advice in days gone by. Most were essentially for the upper classes and what we would now call intellectuals. Pythagoras's followers would not eat beans. Ecclesiastes urges moderation in eating. The sixteenth-century Gallic manuscript *Regimen sanitatis* advises moderation, exercise, a cheerful disposition – and a thrice-daily trip to the lavatory. Luigi Cornaro, the author of *Discorsi della vita sobria* (1558), ended his life consuming eggs and wine, though mostly wine. But it is not till the nineteenth century that Skrabanek finds examples of genuine food lunacy extending to a wider population. Initially, the examples came from the USA. Sylvester Graham was one of the most famous, with his advocacy of bran bread and biscuits. You had to bake your own bread and not eat meat (which induces lust). No coffee, tea or salt; and above all, no masturbation, which causes jaundice, diabetes, acne and bad teeth. His concerns were echoed by Dr John Harvey

Kellogg, the cornflake inventor, who set up in Battle Creek, Michigan, 'a veritable fountainhead of faddism. It became the nation's clearing house for an astonishing array of nostrums, messianic food promoters, millionaire cranks and international quacks' (Ronald Deutsch, *The Nuts Among the Berries* (Ballantine Books, 1961)).

## THE NAZIS AND FOOD FADDISM

Battle Creek in the USA exemplified the way in which various other lunacies were linked to food faddism. The most succinct example in England was the late nineteenth century's Fellowship of the New Life, which was for 'atheists, spiritualists, individualists...communists, anarchists, vegetarians, anti-vivisectionists and anti-vaccinationists'. An even more sinister association of food faddism, and especially vegetarianism, is analysed by Robert Proctor in his *The Nazi War on Cancer* (Princeton University Press, 1999). The emphasis of healthism on manipulating the health of the whole population (rather than curing individuals' diseases) had obvious appeal for the Nazis. Hitler was a vegetarian, although, like many, he did make exceptions for himself. So were Hess, who was also keen on homeopathy and herbal remedies, and Himmler, who was anti tobacco and alcohol and pro fibre. He launched one of the first national healthist campaigns against corpulence in the SS – he also opposed them eating non-natural honey – and ordered the concentration camps to have herb gardens. It is often the case that those experts who do not agree with the food healthist propaganda today in England are accused of being in league with the food companies. The food industry is, of course, the guilty party as far as many of the ideologues and nutters are concerned. They dearly want it to be controlled and regulated. On that subject, here is Himmler (quoted by Proctor):

> *We are in the hands of the food companies, whose*
> *economic clout and advertising make it possible for*
> *them to prescribe what we can and cannot eat.*
> *City folk, living through the winter largely on canned*
> *food are already at their mercy, but now they attack*
> *the countryside with their refined flour, sugar and*
> *white bread. The war has interrupted these proceedings;*
> *after the war we shall take energetic steps to prevent*
> *the ruin of our people by the food industries.*

A final instance of how dotty ideas go together comes in a book, *The Sexual Politics of Meat* by Carol Adams (Polity Press, 1990). Her subtitle says it all – *A Feminist-Vegetarian Critical Theory.* In the early pages Ms Adams trawls through history and finds that many prominent vegetarians were – would you believe? – feminists, and many feminists turn out to have been vegetarians. Moreover, many of these feminist-vegetarians were also socialists and lesbians, and many social-ists and lesbians, it transpires, were feminists and vegetarians! The second part advances Ms Adams's thesis that you can't be a pukka feminist/ socialist/ vegetarian/ lesbian unless you are all the others. Eating meat, she explains, is really like rape. She concludes the book with the haunting phrase, 'Eat Rice Have Faith in Women'.

So what, so far, have we got? An exaggerated concern for food and health is not the rule in western history, but rather the exception. It is found especially in the nineteenth century and after in the Anglo-Saxon rather than the Latin countries. (Hitler was unable to persuade Mussolini of the virtues of veg-etarianism.) Why? The reason why dietary mania occurs in modern societies is that they have sufficient food and enough time and money to fret about what would otherwise be minor concerns. As for why this happens in specifically the Anglo-Saxon countries, rather than the Latin countries, the simple answer is that these have weak food cultures. That means that affluence is likely to lead to unbalanced eating – there are genuine problems of obesity, for instance – but it also leads to unbalanced ideas about diet. In short, the presence of so much hysteria over health and diet, and the willingness of the media to see food as a health, rather than as an eating matter, is evidence of a culture that still can't cook.

## THE DECLINE OF THE FAMILY

But there is more. As Carol Adams reminds us, one can be dotty about things other than food. And these lunacies can have an impact on the way a society eats. If there is an -ism that has really damaged England's eating habits, it is that combination of feminism and sixties 'immoralism' that has broken up so many English families. Traditional good cooking and eating require the passing on of skills from one generation to another; the commitment by one adult member of the family to cook daily; and for that family to stay together. Put simply, the traditional family is the cornerstone of traditional cooking and eating. The commitment and the family within which it was exercised are now largely a thing of the past. Cooking disciplines are not passed from generation to generation because the modern mother has other interests. Traditional eating disciplines are not passed on to children because, under the progressive child-rearing ideology, they are indulged. The last hundred years have, indeed, been the years of ideology – so many ideologies! – and the food culture in England, which was not particularly strong anyway, has been far too weak to withstand the manifold dottiness.

So let us see what the ideologies actually do to cooking and eating – not in theoretical terms, but to actual meals. As I have repeatedly stressed, breakfast was one of the few really good things in English cooking before the so-called 'food revolutions' of the last forty years. Visiting foreigners, even the French, would despair of most food but would lavish praise on *le breakfast*. We have already mentioned boiled eggs, but the staple English breakfast was green or smoked bacon, fried eggs, toast – made with white bread – butter, marmalade or Marmite, and tea with sugar and full-cream milk. Variations included fried pork or beef sausages, fried bread, fried tomatoes, *sauté* potatoes, bubble and squeak, baked beans, fried mushrooms and, in the North, black pudding. Occasionally there were kippers or herrings.

## WHAT THE -ISMS DO TO BREAKFAST

The current obsession of healthists is with salt. They urge a drastic reduction in salt to combat heart disease. The bacon will have to go, and so will the sausages, the kippers and the black pudding. The sausages and black pudding have not only salt, but evil nitrates. One may eat an egg, but only once a week on account of the cholesterol. The egg should not be fried, as it traditionally was, in pork or beef fat; in fact, it shouldn't really be fried at all. The concerns over fat would certainly do for the bubble and squeak and *sauté* potatoes, which soaked up gallons of the stuff. Marmite has far too much salt. Butter should be replaced with some sort of spread without animal fats, and the milk in the tea should be skimmed. Baked beans would be permissible, but only without the sugar and salt they traditionally contain. Herrings are fine but should not be consumed often (dioxins). Tomatoes are good, too, but should be grilled. Toast should be made not with white bread, but with something heavy, brown and with straw sticking out of it. Fried bread is anathema.

There is only one word to describe what healthism does to the English breakfast. It *destroys* it. It renders the meal impossible except as an occasional indulgent treat. The healthists can go on all they like about not wanting to be bossy, and only encouraging sensible eating; about the joys of muesli and prunes. But the truth is clear. The one meal that was a joy to eat in England is not allowed under their 'healthy diet'. I suppose they might reply – the few half-honest ones among them

– that this is indeed the case. And they might add that there are other good breakfasts to be had. Other countries enjoy their own breakfasts. Why don't we copy them? This, of course, evades the fact that visitors from those other countries envied the traditional English breakfast and enjoyed it more than their own.

But there is another point. What are these 'other' breakfasts? One of them is of special interest, given that the healthists rant on about the virtues of a Mediterranean 'diet'. Go into any bar in Spain and watch what these Mediterranean people are eating. They like coffee with lots of milk, some of it sweet and condensed. Each dose of coffee is accompanied by 'refined' sugar, drained from a sachet that is expertly flicked open so that it empties entirely. On the bar are bowls of pork liver *pâté* (50 per cent fat), butter, fat with paprika and plain pork fat. Behind the bar is one of those incredibly inefficient toasting machines that can never keep up with demand. The customers have toasted ultra-white bread, loaded with *pâté*, fat or olive oil and then tuck into very sweet *croissants* – with lots of meat fat in them – and assorted pastries. If the bar is in or near a market they might also have omelette or tripe with salty sausage of one sort or another, or maybe some salt cod or snails. With breakfast they enjoy a cigarette, and sometimes a brandy or anise. None of this fits the so-called 'Mediterranean diet'. Indeed, the principle holds true for many other dishes in Spain and France, and for meals other than breakfast. In these days of cheap airlines, everyone has been to the Mediterranean: no, not everyone, not the healthists. They simply do not know what they are talking about. Anyway, the upshot is this: to fit their ideals, the white toast, the *pâté* with its fat and salt, the fat, the frequent omelettes, the *callos* (tripe) with its fat and salt, the sweet pastries, the Marlboros, the brandy and the condensed milk will all have to go. Not content with destroying the English breakfast, they would like to destroy the Spanish one as well. These unpleasant people constantly insinuate themselves as moderate and reasonable, only wanting the population to make minor adjustments to what they eat. As with the claims of the vegetarians, it is just not true.

## WHAT THE -ISMS DO TO LUNCH AND DINNER

It is not merely breakfast that they would wreck. Take some of the best dishes in French and Latin cuisines. Consider a few lunch or dinner menus:

*Menu*

Assorted *charcuterie*
*Brandade de morue*
*Plateau de fromages*
Fruit
Coffee

*Menu*

*Pâtes à l'anchois*
*Coq au vin*
Cheese, fruit, coffee

*Menu*

*Artichauts vinaigrette*
*Blanquette de veau*
Cheese, fruit, coffee

These are scarcely extravagant menus, either in cost or taste. They are solid, established and widespread French meals. I could have produced dozens more from *choucroute*, *steak-frites*, *pot-au-feu*, *jambon cru*, *tomates farcies*, *salade Niçoise* to brains or skate in black butter. Break them down. The assorted *charcuterie* consists of *rillettes* of duck, *pâté* and *saucisson*. The *rillettes* and pork are 50 per cent fat, the *saucisson* slightly less. All have a fair amount of salt in them.

*Brandade* is made of soaked, poached salt cod (salt again) blended with full cream milk, olive oil and garlic. One quite usual and very good accompaniment is white bread fried in olive oil. The cheese board might have *Roquefort* (tons of salt), *chèvre* and *Camembert*. The *chèvre* and *Camembert* are 45 per cent fat. The meal is accompanied by an ordinary white baguette and wine. None of it is permissible under the healthist code.

The pastry which contains the anchovies itself contains fat and the anchovies are very salty. As to the *blanquette de veau* – I quote from Simone Beck *et al.*, *Mastering the Art of French Cooking* (Penguin, 1961), with added emphasis, 'a *much loved stew in France*, is veal simmered in a lightly seasoned white stock...served in a sauce enriched with *cream and egg yolks*'. In all, 2.5 ounces of butter are required and just under half a pint of cream. The authors recommend it be served with mashed potatoes, which, of course, require lots more butter and cream. If these quantities make the healthists blanch rather than tremble, do not forget that this is but one course in a meal with at least two others, and that it is only lunch. Dinner is another matter.

As one goes north in France the quantities of cream and butter increase. Further south the problem – for the healthists – is salt, and everywhere there is dairy fat and meat fat. Even the comparatively innocent *coq au vin* is thickened with *beurre manié* and has *lardons*. There is just no way to squeeze or misrepresent the cuisine of France to fit within the diet approved by the healthists. The same is true of Spain and Portugal, and indeed of Italy or even China. The healthists are at war with the best of food in the world.

## SATISFY ONE -ISM AND YOU RUN FOUL OF ANOTHER

I chose the third menu for a special reason. It looks the nearest to healthism, for healthists approve of artichokes. True, they are not as dull (and thus worthy) as broccoli, or as tasteless as the squash family, but still they are permissible. As indeed is *coq au vin*, if not the cheese that follows or the quantities of white bread dunked in the sauce. However, the healthists are not the only censors to whom we have to submit our menu. I maintain that a really good *coq au vin* wants to be not some adolescent cockerel or young chicken, but a mature bird. These are now very difficult to find in English butchers. They are, to be sure, readily available from halal establishments. However, they will have been killed without having first been stunned, and no one who follows the sentimental creeds of today's urban animal-rights enthusiasts could contemplate eating such a bird.

Artichokes are not (yet) believed to feel pain. However, the best will have been imported from Brittany and, in the process, will have used up fuels and caused environmental damage. So the environmental conscience cannot accept them. In any case, yet other activists are on hand to remind us of our duty to buy fresh produce locally – not only to avoid environmental damage, but to support our small farmers against the evil food industry. Quite what local, fresh vegetables we are supposed to buy in January I have never discovered. Is it to be sprouts every day? Or do swedes stored for ages count as fresh?

## THE COMBINED EFFECT OF THE NUTTERS

The animal sentimentalists, the environmentalists and the localists would, no doubt, like to stick their oar into the other menus, too. They regard veal as very wicked. Salt cod is made from a fish that has been over-fished, and they would like to stop it being caught. The combined efforts of the various food lobbies leave precious little that is good to eat. In theory, though, the -isms are not always joined up. Thus, for instance, the healthists *might* allow us an occasional pork sausage for breakfast if it did not contain too much salt or fat. And there is a way to ensure this. The healthists say that excessive fat is often found in processed foods. If, as most sensible people do, we all made our own sausages, we could reduce the salt and the fat. To do this we need to be able to buy pork from older, fatter pigs. That is where the taste is, and some fat (20 per cent as a minimum) is required for a good sausage. Unfortunately, the food safety people and the healthists have so affected both the supply and the demand for pork that the pigs that are easily available are killed far too young.

The assorted ideologues and nutters affect the national diet, then – not only directly but by their influence on the population's shopping, cooking and eating habits. There is often a curious symbiosis here. For instance, for a long time people who were squeamish or childish about food had to put up with being reprimanded or scorned for being squeamish or childish. Now they can hide the moral failing under modern virtues: 'No jellied eels for me! I read that there is now a shortage, so responsible people are not eating eels this year.'

The overall effect of the various food ideologies, when added to native inclinations such as squeamishness, is to fuel fear of, and aversion to, good food. One way or another, the ideologues provide a variety of reasons for rejecting the best dishes to have evolved in the best cuisines in the world. And what would they put in their place?

### PRECAUTIONS TO TAKE WHEN APPROACHING A SAUSAGE

There are healthy-eating missionaries who do not go as far as the healthists. They do not lie about the 'joys' of healthy eating. But neither do they acknowledge how dull and ugly the healthy diet is. They are rightly shocked by junk food but seem unaware how many good things their own diet forbids. Consider, for instance, the foods one well-known nutritionist (Jane Clarke, *The Times*, 5 November 2005) suggests for teenagers: wholegrain cereals, muesli, porridge, wholemeal bread, pasta with tomato and vegetable sauces (low salt no doubt), dried fruits for snacks, tortilla wraps (I suppose low fat) stuffed with houmous, vegetable curries, yoghurt, chicken breasts, tofu, lentils and (dried) beans, and lots of water. It would be difficult to parody this. Unlike the vegetarians, Ms Clarke and many of the healthists are kind enough to allow us proper food occasionally, as a special indulgence. But only if ritual precautions are observed. Here is what you have to do before you can nibble a sausage sandwich – that is, a sandwich with a single sausage (*The Times*, 12 November 2005). You must choose a brand with 80 per cent meat, cook it on a raised grill (to allow the fat to drip off), and wipe it with paper (so that not a drop of outside fat enters the mouth). You are also allowed the occasional piece of pork crackling. It has to be 'a little', though, and 'occasional', just as a 'treat'. Ms Clarke is kind enough to assure us that 'there is nothing wrong' in eating this. But she urges us to make sure the rest of our lunch is high in fibre, with non-buttered, non-oiled vegetables and 'maybe' boiled or steamed potatoes. Thank you, Jane, and I promise to go to the gym as well.

# CHAPTER 10

# CONCLUSION: A CULTURE THAT STILL CAN'T COOK

## THOSE FOOD REVOLUTIONS

Modern English people like to think that the food in their country is rather good. They admit that it was not always so, but claim that there have been successive revolutions in the way we eat at home and in restaurants, as well as in the food available in our shops and markets. More generally, it is claimed that our food culture has changed. We congratulate ourselves on knowing more about food and on being more interested in it. *The Times* for instance, has declared that 'the national palate [is becoming] more discerning' (9 January 2006). Indeed, it is said that, while it used to be rather disapproved of to show an interest in food, now food itself and discussion of it are widespread sources of pleasure.

All of this is nonsense. Each claim is not only false but manifestly so. Simply look at what is being eaten, not just occasionally but daily, in homes, restaurants, hospitals, schools, at airports, on planes, trains and beaches, on the pavements, in offices, at corporate receptions and in university halls and digs: not only is this daily food not good – it is awful. The food of the pre-revolutionary fifties, so derided today, was indeed largely dull and insular, but at least there was an abundance of butchers and fishmongers with locally produced food, and Englishwomen shopped at them and cooked thrice-daily meals, which their families ate together, sitting down. The same *Times* article cited above cheerfully admits that 'we now spend an average of just 13 minutes a day preparing food, compared with 60 minutes in the Eighties'. Instead of making even a minimum effort to cook and eat decently, we spend £12.3 billion a year on snacks (the same *Times* article again). Some discernment.

## NEW TRENDS IN BAD FOOD

There have been changes for the better: a much wider variety of foods is available in shops and there are a few better (but very expensive) restaurants. However, there have been far more changes for the worse: a deluge of second-rate industrial cheeses, meats and vegetables and third-rate takeaways, fast-food outlets and formulaic 'Indians' and Chinese. Worst of all, the institution of the family, so vital to the provision of good food and the transfer of knowledge about it, has collapsed in an orgy of self-indulgent sexual and emotional relationships and a decline in unifying behaviour and values. So busy are its members chasing higher incomes or each other's partners, conspicuously consuming and satisfying their individual 'rights' and tastes that meals are not regularly cooked or eaten together.

A new list of obstacles to good cooking and eating has emerged. There are vegetarians who reject whole classes of foods that wiser civilizations have produced and valued, healthists who reduce food to a mere tool in the manic pursuit of another few years of miserable life on earth, environmentalists who subject good eating to their dotty political cause, health-safety lobbyists who stifle good food in their regulations. Even more important are the refusal to make the daily effort necessary to produce good meals, the transformation of eating into an excuse for showing off, and the relentless pursuit of novelty and celebrity. Some of these obstacles to good food are genuinely new – the aversion to effort, for instance: the fifties housewife worked hard shopping and in the kitchen. But underlying some of the other new obstacles are old tendencies, above all the rejection of large numbers of fine ingredients or dishes on one spurious ground or another:

squeamishness and insipidity, the fear of the unfamiliar and the hope that profusion – notably in vegetables – will substitute for one good item cooked properly.

Most of all, the national self-congratulators are wrong about the change in food culture. Modern English people are not interested in food. That is, they are not interested enough to make the effort, to subject themselves to the shopping, eating and cooking disciplines that are the proof of true commitment. This is manifest in the way that food is written about and read and talked about. The words of English food-talk are froth. Dishes are found 'wonderful' or 'dreadful', but no one can describe why. There is no vocabulary of good food, because there are no deep and agreed standards on which to base such a vocabulary.

### BACK TO BREAKFAST – AGAIN: LOOK AT WHO REJECTS IT

Consider a few examples of these points. To see that rejectionism is not confined to the old, dull, narrow English cooking but lives today, we return (yet again) to breakfast. The English have rejected most of the good things of breakfast, from kidneys to smoked haddock, for most of the time. Some of them reject them 365 days a year. Day after day they spurn them. They have a bit of toast or a bowl of cereal instead. The people who reject these good things are not necessarily stupid, impoverished, ill-educated or common. In a survey of eating, the *Independent* (6 September 2001) revealed that Trevor Morris, 46, the chairman of the Good Relations Group of seven public companies, has a cup of coffee at home with a banana, followed by a bagel with Marmite at a café. Not a mention of fried rabbit or haddock. Why not? He can afford them. He must know about them. Sophie Grigson is the daughter of Jane Grigson, author of one of the best books on pork and *charcuterie* cooking. My copy of her mother's best book can scarcely be opened, so stuck together are the pages with the blood from liver, so flecked are they by the tiny bits of bone spattered on them when splitting the pig's head to get at the brain. Sophie is a well-published food expert herself. So what does Sophie have for breakfast? (Remember, this is just one generation on.) She has a cup of tea, organic muesli with fruit and semi-skimmed milk (*Sunday Telegraph*, 1 August 2004). I don't know whether Jane ate breakfast with Sophie, but nowadays less than a third of people do sit down to it with their children, a half eat it alone, and a third skip it altogether. Some people constantly, even manically, reject proper breakfasts every day. Others, even more puzzlingly, select one good dish and have it every day. Thus the *Times* columnist Giles Coren (2 July 2005) eats two poached eggs 'every morning'. He, like Mr Morris, has it at a café. Why? Why would anyone with taste want 14 café-poached eggs every week, 728 café-poached eggs a year, and reject kidneys and mackerel? What sort of example is this to set young people who are only too ready to conform to any lazy habit on offer? And a café-poached egg! The best cafés can be trusted with black pudding (just), but not poached eggs. Do cafés have duck eggs? It must be duck eggs Mr Coren is referring to, for two hen's eggs would only satisfy an anti-cholesterol fanatic. Yet nobody wrote to *The Times* to express astonishment or indignation at such a bizarre spurning of good food.

## QUESTIONABLE STATEMENTS ABOUT FOOD GO UNCORRECTED AND UNCHALLENGED

The absence of such letters in response to food writing is particularly significant. Food journalists write much that is of questionable taste. Occasionally they are also factually incorrect or just plain ignorant. Yet few letters appear correcting them. Either no one notices, or else the editors do not think readers are interested enough to read such corrections. It boils down to the same thing: a nation that is ignorant about, or not seriously interested in, food. Some newspapers do solicit enquiries from readers about food problems. These, together with the responses, are highly instructive. Thus, one such enquiry was about mutton. The reader wanted to buy mutton but could not find any. Where could she track some down? The newspaper's food expert replied that mutton was, indeed, very rare but that he/she had managed to find some on a website. Since the 1960s England has enjoyed much immigration from the Indian subcontinent, and many of these immigrants have been Muslims. Newspapers comment on them quite frequently, and they can be identified in the streets on account of their distinctive clothing. They are hard-working, skilful traders and now run many shops. These shops stock three main meats – chicken, lamb and mutton, prominently labelled – and there are thousands of such shops. Mutton is more freely available than ever. How can the readers and the experts be so blind?

## WHAT FOOD CELEBRITIES THEMSELVES EAT

Back (yet again) to breakfast and the food-spurners. An article in the *Sunday Telegraph* does not quite make it clear whether Nigella Lawson, popularly known as a food-goddess, always eats the same way, but on the day she was asked, it would seem, she had rejected everything save one boiled egg (28 May 2005). It is hardly surprising: this is a person who eats her dinner in bed in front of the television and includes in it broccoli! At least she sits down properly at lunch. The food writer Mary Berry, who has written a book with the predictable but depressing title *Real Food: Fast* (Headline, 2005) seems quite unabashed when she admits that Christmas is 'the one day of the year when we use the dining-room table' (*Daily Telegraph*, 23 December 2005). And even on Christmas Day she can't rise to a proper breakfast: just toast, *croissants* and fruit. Mind you, this is someone who cooks turkey 'because it goes an awfully long way'. What an extraordinary reason for choosing a dish.

## HER MAJESTY: LAMB AND SALMON AGAIN

Her Majesty the Queen would seem to be a bit of a rejectionist on the quiet. Having no information on her breakfasts, I refer instead to her dinners. I cannot pretend to have perused the menu for every meal she has had, but whenever I read about her state banquets she always seems to be eating salmon and roast lamb with boring vegetables – too many of them and never as part of a dish. She never permits herself and her guests pigeons stewed in red wine, or fried crab with garlic and ginger, or pigs' ears in jelly, or oxtail and dumplings. The poor Chinese President Hu Jintao was recently given the salmon and roast lamb treatment with – and remember this is a Chinaman, someone who knows his grub, born of a race that rejects nothing in the food line – *carottes nouvelles*, glazed courgettes and a salad of buttermilk squash. Talk about boring for Britain! The point is that these are all people who should be setting an example. So is, or was, Sir John Krebs, until recently the chairman of the Food Standards Agency. Being an English agency, the body is not, of course, about food standards at all. It is not there to promote better food – food of a better standard. It is not there to help people learn to stop eating boring boiled carrots and start loving sweetbreads in butter. However, you might expect him to eat the odd poached tail of smoked haddock for his breakfast or a calorie-controlled portion of kidney. But no, his grinning photo appears next to the public admission that breakfast is muesli and low-fat yoghurt. He grazes on fruit all day. Lunch is a wholemeal sandwich with raw carrot, and dinner chargrilled tuna with – oh, isn't it nauseatingly predictable! – 'griddled courgette' (*Sunday Telegraph*, 21 November 2004). Courgettes might well be the emblem of the new cuisine: watery, pretentious in a dated way, and ubiquitous.

The working title for this book was *The Culture That Still Can't Cook*. I felt, though, that it was not quite right, not least because it implies continuity, whereas, in fact, we see continuity of some bad tendencies and the arrival of some new ones to make matters worse. The actual title, *The English at Table*, is, of course, a bad joke. If the decline in English food continues at its current pace, soon very few English people will even possess a dining table, let alone have the commitment to cook anything worthwhile for it. No doubt they will be congratulating themselves.